Contents

One of the things I'm most proud of as it relates to the whole concept of Connect for Life is the number of people I have helped in their careers. The quotes you see below are just a few of the people who have benefitted from these concepts contained in this book. Many business people judge their success on money or prestige; I judge mine on the people who take their careers to the next level. Many of my friends who buy into these ideas end up running their own companies and for me, this defines my success.

John Humphrey, Founder, Author – Connect for Life

There are many people I know that professionally network but when I think of who defines it, I think of John Humphrey.

Steven Rogers, Founder – ActiveCyber

Everyone needs a coach. John served as a coach for me for several instrumental years. His Connect for Life Framework changed my career trajectory by helping me pivot from a technical manager to a business leader. The approach is not one that will necessarily help you strike overnight success. It is quite the contrary. It is a proven model that stands the test of time based on a simple yet highly underrated concept – helping people. The tactical tips and nuances provided in this book are ones you will be challenged to find in the best networking and relationship books you can find.

Dipesh Patel, Founder – Solvegy

John wrote his book about me, indirectly. We met when he was at Lawson. I was at the end of that dirt road. What I learned from John became a life-long connection. John's ability to love, learn, inspire, and teach is his gift from God for the people of God. Take some time to dive in and use John's Connect for Life handbook to help elevate your life. I promise it works. I consistently refer to his teachings. You will too.

**Mike McGibbony,
Founder – Whiterock Technologies**

I am one of the many students who have benefitted from John's teaching around the Connect for Life concept. I have used John's Connect for Life framework to grow my skills in connecting and my company continues to benefit. I am now both a student and teacher of John's Connect for Life framework.

**Saurajit Kanungo, President – Cyber
Group**

Connect for Life gave me a foundation for sustained and meaningful growth, enriching both personal and business relationships.

**Dbrav Dunkley,
Vice President – Credera**

Introduction

I sat there staring at the phone as though it would make the call by itself.
This was back before the Internet, email, and cell phones, at a time when
appointments were arranged by phone calls, followed by visits to
prospective clients and pitching deals. I was nervous, not trembling, but
had that pit-in-my-stomach feeling you get in anticipation of a major
event, such as a final exam or when your team is in the playoffs. *What
would they say? What would they think of me? What if they said "no"?*
So, I did what any other rookie sales person would do; I shuffled the
papers on my desk, paced around the office, and took a trip to the
restroom-anything to keep from making that call. When I finally reached
the point where I could no longer procrastinate, I knew I was ready. I
dialed the number and the phone started ringing. My mind raced all over
again. *What would I say? What if they didn't answer? Oh crap, I hadn't
thought about that!* The phone rang and rang. *Should I leave a
message? Should I hang up? What should I say?* I quickly hung up,
dejected, a failure.

This selling stuff was tough. I hated it already, and I hadn't even
spoken to one person. I had only dialed one phone number, yet my
palms were sweaty, my shirt pitted out, and my heart was pounding
inside my chest. Next, I did another rookie thing. I straightened my
desk...again, walked around the office, got a Coke, and returned to my

desk. I dialed the same number again but this time I thought I was ready for someone to answer. They didn't. As I heard the "leave a message beep," time stood still. Words formed in my head, but what came out of my mouth sounded something like, "Um, um, hi Mr. Jones, (long pause), um, this is um, John, um, Humphrey with Computron Software, (another long pause). I was wondering if…"

Then suddenly I was interrupted by a loud beep followed by, "If you are satisfied with your message, press 1, if you would like to delete and re-record press 2…"

My mind was racing. *Was I supposed to press 1 or 2?* Then, beep! I quickly pressed 1 and instead of being able to re-record I heard, "Thank you for your message," a click and then nothing. I sat there for a moment staring at the phone feeling as if I wanted to throw up. *Oh crap, did I even say my name?* I slammed down the phone, collected my briefcase, and walked out the door. What a day!

I remember thinking on the drive home that there had to be a better way. I had always been rich in friends and relationships, and it suddenly occurred to me that maybe somebody in my network might know the CFO at the company with whom I was trying to get a meeting. So, the next day, I started paging through my Rolodex (this was before LinkedIn), and calling my contacts and friends. After a bit of catching up on the phone with each of these folks, I eventually got around to asking

the question, "Do you know anyone at (fill in the blank) company?" Most didn't but a few did, and eventually I landed a meeting without having to rely on a cold call. What a relief!

Sometimes when you start a journey, the destination is the only goal, the end, not the journey. The epiphany I experienced on this journey was that my friends and colleagues needed help along the road, too--perhaps a new car, a new banking relationship, a realtor, a good lawyer, etc. I realized that the value of the connection was mutually beneficial; I could help others as well by *lending* them my contacts. What started as a fear-induced way to avoid cold calls became the avocation of my life.

This book is designed for any knowledge worker who has wondered how they can be more effective at networking and selling in their careers. It is the shortcut to understanding how they can leverage all the knowledge capital that they have amassed in solving problems for others. If you are a developer, an engineer, a senior architect, a lawyer, an accountant, or any other type of knowledge worker and you wonder why the sales guy gets the credit for the work that you created, then this book can assist you in becoming a trusted advisor.

Because my background is in technology consulting, there is a technical slant to the audience I address in this book, but anyone in sales can benefit from *Connect for Life*. We will cover the basics of connecting

and the under-the-cover reasons for how and why reciprocity works in today's knowledge-driven economy. Then we will transition to evaluating a system called Touch Points that will help you understand how meaningful networking activity leads to success in life. We will cover how to move beyond networking to connecting and building meaningful relationships that will serve you for the rest of your life.

Finally, we will examine both internal and external enterprise selling and describe how, as a knowledge worker, you can be in control of your future whether you want to start your own company or improve your income by staying at another's company. A major component of connecting for life is giving, since giving of yourself results in business success. By following the *Connect for Life* system, you can unlock your talents in the marketplace and find fulfillment beyond what you have achieved to this point in your career.

When I look back on my upbringing, I have always worked toward the *Connect for Life* philosophy. I was raised in an upper-middle-class household by educated parents who expected me to give my very best, to treat everyone with respect and dignity, and to be trustworthy and reliable. From a young age, I wanted to work for myself. I watched my friends toil as grocery stockers or paper boys, and it always seemed more advantageous to be independent. As a teenager, I always had a dollar in my pocket whether from mowing lawns or painting houses and

fences, or being a handy man for hire. This was my first exposure to networking and connecting. Where did these jobs come from? They came from people I knew and those who knew what I was doing. They facilitated the introduction, or in a passing statement they said, "Hey, I know a guy who painted my fence. Let me give you his number." Even before I could drive myself around town, my mom was toting me around with a lawnmower in the back of the family Chevy Nova. When my other industrious friends went on a family vacation, I mowed their clients' lawns, and when I was out of town, they did likewise for me. I learned to be a trustworthy person of my word.

As time passed, I began to think about colleges, I decided I wanted to go to school in the South. My family had spent summers at the beach in Georgia, and I loved it there. Living in New Jersey during my childhood, I saw many of my friends' dads walking to the train station in the morning and commuting into New York City. I knew that was not for me, so I put a list together of good schools in the South and went on a family road trip between my junior and senior year in high school. During this search, a friend of mine who was attending Texas Christian University (TCU) in Fort Worth, Texas, brought me a brochure for Southern Methodist University (SMU) in Dallas, Texas. SMU was not on my list but fit all my criteria. It was in a large, quickly growing Southern city known for its friendly people. While not in the Southeast (my favored

location), it seemed like a natural. My father's brother lived in Austin, and that made me feel like I was close to family. Having my uncle in Texas proved to be very comforting during some trying times in college, especially over Thanksgiving.

Suddenly, just like that, I was a Texan. I even wore a cowboy hat the summer after my senior year of high school. Texas was a long way from northern New Jersey, but there I was hugging my mom and dad goodbye at Newark International Airport. They bought me a ticket and gave me some money and off I went on a flight. When I arrived, I took the Super Shuttle to the Hilton Hotel on the corner of Central Expressway and Mockingbird Lane and walked the rest of the way onto campus lugging my two suitcases. It was the summer of 1980, the hottest on record. The entire way, I questioned my decision, thinking, "I have died and gone to hell, it's so hot." When I arrived at my dorm I was dripping in sweat and about to begin a new adventure a long way from home.

I often tell this story tongue-in-cheek, that I got a plane ticket and a quarter, and my parents said, "Call us when you get there." That wasn't far from the truth. I remember not thinking anything about it as I was going off to school and becoming independent. Nowadays, for most high school grads arriving at college, it is a two-car process plus a U-Haul attached to one vehicle. Back then, not so much. Still, I knew my family

loved me and would always be there for me. This was my real first test of independence, and I was ready.

I was not the only member of my family who had walked alone into a new adventure. I remember hearing stories about how my father walked to Grand Central Station as a young teenager, by himself, to board a train for college. I guess that was just how my family rolled. "You're on your own kid, good luck! Call if you need anything!"

My family had the entrepreneurial gene on both sides. My father's father, Harold J. Humphrey, graduated from Cornell University in 1917, and was a food chemist for the United States Department of Agriculture (USDA) until he went to work for Snider Packing Company in 1926. Soon thereafter, he was offered the chance to become the president of the National Canning Association. At the time, Snider was experimenting with a new frozen food process and despite having eight manufacturing facilities around greater New York that were engaged in canning, Harold Humphrey felt he would be put in a compromising position to take the offer, so he declined. Snider's expertise was canning tomatoes and peas and making catsup and chili sauce.

The migration to frozen foods happened slowly. In 1929, Birds Eye was purchased by Postum Company and Goldman Sachs for $22 million and the new company was named General Foods. One of Birdseye's inventions was the Birdseye multiplate freezer, which Snider

eventually licensed from General Foods. What General Foods soon

learned was that the packaging process was difficult and important.

Snider had created a better way of processing frozen vegetables so that

they kept their taste and structure and by the early 1930's they were

using the Birdseye technology at the Snider plant in Albion, New York.

My grandfather thought that it was a pretty good idea and if Snider

continued production, eventually General Foods might acquire them. At

least that was the thinking.

My father recalls conversations around the breakfast table about

"the loan." In the first major investments of my grandfather's life, he took

everything their household could spare, plus all the money the bank

would lend them, and they invested in stock for the Snider Packing

Corporation. Like many entrepreneurial stories, history looks at the

results of these decisions, not the difficult preliminary conversations

around the breakfast table announcing to your family your plans to bet it

all on an opportunity. It was not only a bold and gutsy decision, but also

took perseverance to wait more than 10 years to see if it would work. It

did work, and my grandfather is chronicled in history for playing a key

role in the frozen food revolution. He retired in 1959 and became a

consultant for United Nations Children's Fund (UNICEF). In 1962 he

developed a global nutrition plan for children. To be a part of that food

revolution was exhilarating, difficult, uncertain and very rewarding for my grandfather. His was a life well-lived.

J. Paul Humphrey, my father, followed in his father's entrepreneurial footsteps when in 1973, he quit his job at Standard Packaging to become a stockbroker at age 42. He had a mortgage and three children, and off he went!! For those of you who know U.S. economic history, this was a very difficult economic period. With soaring inflation and high unemployment, it was certainly not the best environment for starting a business. Many refer to this period as the worst stagflation (a period of high inflation and low growth) since the great depression. Paul Humphrey started with a vision of helping people manage their financial assets, a long list of friends and contacts, a high level of integrity, a telephone, and a typewriter. As an eleven-year old, I remember the family's financial hardships as my mom went to work and my elder sisters both had after-school jobs. My major hardship was not having chocolate chip cookies after school, so it was relatively easy on me. I also remember my sister and dad working late every night typing letters and envelopes to contacts, friends, and family encouraging them to trust J. Paul Humphrey with their financial assets. It was my first encounter where both connecting, and trust united with a considerable amount of work. My dad continues today to be an avid investor at the ripe old age of 85.

My career began at Texas American Bancshares in Fort Worth, Texas, after graduating from SMU in 1984 with a double major in Finance and Economics. While a double major may sound impressive, I can't take credit for it. My best friend in college figured out one day that we had both taken many hours of economics courses, which was in the Dedman College, not the Cox School of Business at SMU, where we were taking our general business classes. He said, "You know, if we take a little summer school, we can get out of here in four years with two degrees." I was in.

That college experience was a fitting example of the notion of surrounding yourself with good people and growing old with them. He and I are still fast friends today, both of us members in a duck club, and investors together in several real estate ventures. Growing old with good people is part of the secret of success that everyone should be chasing. We parlayed that idea into a study abroad program in Oxford, England. What a great memory, as well as a fun and adventurous summer.

In 1984 I entered the real world and became a credit analyst at Texas American Bancshares, Inc. I met regularly with senior lenders and the executives at the bank, learned how to spread financial statements, and was exposed to a wide range of different businesses and industries. Back then an analyst had to become a quick study on different business models and learn how to analyze the highlights quickly for the loan

officers and then articulate those ideas well in a loan committee package.

From a social perspective, I found a church and was soon part of the team leading song worship for the high school group. My relationships expanded, and one day a parent of one of my church students asked me if I had any interest in becoming an entrepreneur. As a naïve young man, I said, "Of course, do you have something in mind?" The father was the president of Sweetshop Candy Corporation in Fort Worth. He and one of his partners had invested in Sweet Shop and Pangburn Candy companies, and they had an interest in getting into the retail food business. I was in.

We found a steakhouse franchise that was for sale in Burleson, Texas. After working through the details over a period of months, there I sat on a Friday afternoon at the closing dressed in my dark blue banker suit and white shirt. I left the closing and went down to the restaurant as a 10% owner and general manager of the store, knowing very little about the food business. The former owner informed the staff of the change in ownership, and my entrepreneurial adventure began. The next four years would find me working seven days a week, having the number of stores expand to four with one in Burleson, Texas, one in Cleburne, Texas, and two in different parts of Fort Worth. It was my first encounter with failure. We went from one to four restaurants and back to one in about three

years. We had brought in another partner in the middle of our expansion who ended up with a significant amount of the debt load. Over the years, we became fast friends. There is nothing like a crisis to bond people together over time. I have the utmost respect for how he handled that challenge of repaying the debt that he had to pay back after our restaurant enterprise failed. He faced it head-on and over the next 20 years paid all the money back without a harsh word. What an example of a man standing by his commitment.

So, there I was at the age of 27, making $30,000 a year, recently married, and $250,000 in debt. I was totally burned out. If not for my relationship with my partners, I would have been totally wiped out. They saved me in more ways than they know. I was able to negotiate a sale of my remaining interest to one partner and paid back a much smaller amount than I owed, then parlayed that experience into a shot at graduate school at the Cox School of Business at Southern Methodist University. That one partner had given me a gift of debt forgiveness that I will never forget. It would not be the last favor that someone bestowed on me and planted in me the seed of passing that gratitude on to others. With that gift, he made a huge investment in me and became a life-long mentor and friend.

At that time, SMU offered a one-year Master in Business Administration degree. Graduate school was a great experience wrapped

in a challenging year where I forged many friendships and learned a great deal. Because of my recent business failure experience, I dove into accounting, finance, marketing, and entrepreneurial courses and they became more relevant than ever. I could not get enough.

Upon graduating with my M.B.A., I went to work for a technology start-up called BancA, a Ross Perot venture. I met the CEO of BancA because he was a member of the SMU Associate Board, a mentoring and coaching association for graduate students. Another one of the founders of BancA became one of my life-long friends and mentors as I shared various entrepreneurial ideas with her over the years. I remember her telling me that it was just as important to define what you are not going to do as it is to define what you are going to do.

The rollercoaster ride of a venture start-up, going from feast to famine, eventually led to BancA being sold to a company known then as Andersen Consulting, where I met one of my future partners. It was because of our plans to start a company together that I later left Andersen Consulting. I would be sales and marketing, and he would be the financial and technical guy. The only problem was that I had never actually been in direct sales. So, in 2005 I called one of my former colleagues from BancA, who had left a while before and was now a sales manager for Computron, an enterprise accounting software firm. As luck would have it, he had an opening. He hired me into my first

commissioned sales position, even though I had never "carried a bag" or sold directly to the market. I was as clueless in my first sales meeting at Computron as I was on the Friday evening that I showed up at the steakhouse. I followed my nose, attempted to learn fast, and tried really hard not to say anything stupid.

I tell you all these connection stories because the themes of relationships--trust, integrity, faith, and perseverance--are woven through the tapestry of my life, and the essence of this book is to unlock those concepts and ideas, so you can put things together sooner than I did. I didn't even really put it together at Computron. A friend of mine had a brother-in-law whom I had met on a few occasions. He was an account executive at Lawson Software, an enterprise resource planning (ERP) software company. ERP is a fancy term that encompasses accounting, order entry, inventory management, and distribution software. He got me an interview and I got the job at Lawson and left Computron. Almost an entire year passed before I sold my first deal. I really thought I would be fired because I was competing in downtown Dallas with the likes of SAP, Peoplesoft, JD Edwards, and Oracle. It was the late 1990s, the era of the famous Y2K race where companies were racing the clock to replace their enterprise systems. My boss at Lawson was a great guy and a magnificent sales person. He had previously worked in the Dallas office for Lawson, which was one of the top offices in the U.S. When I sat down

with him after banging my head against the wall and asked him to tell me what I was doing wrong, he would say. "Just keep doing what you are doing."

One day out of frustration, I called our regional executive and asked him if we could go to lunch. I remember sitting at this little Mexican restaurant in North Dallas asking him if he had any recommendations. He asked me about the deals I had lost so I recanted this deal and that deal and he finally said to me, "You know John, Lawson runs best at the end of a dirt road." What the heck was that supposed to mean, I wondered? He went on to tell me that I was competing in the glass towers in Dallas against the top competitors, and those companies were less interested in low total cost of ownership and easy implementations. You see, one of the advantages that Lawson had in the marketplace was that their product didn't take a legion of consultants working for Big 5 consulting firms to implement the software. While other software vendors might cost two or three times in consulting services of what the software license was, Lawson was typically less than one to one. He said, "Go find some distributors outside of Dallas who are small enough to care about price and large enough to afford what we have to offer. Boom! All of a sudden, I was in. Over the next three years my personal income went up 50 percent each year and, every year. This anecdote highlights the importance of seeking out mentors and coaches who can help you,

especially if it means having them tell you something that you don't want to hear. These stories also highlight the importance of not quitting. If you put forth the effort and ask for help, you will generally get where you are going.

During my time at Lawson, the genesis of *Connect for Life* was born. While I was successful at using my relationships and contacts to get into the right companies, I was also victim of the sales person's dilemma depicted in the graphic below.

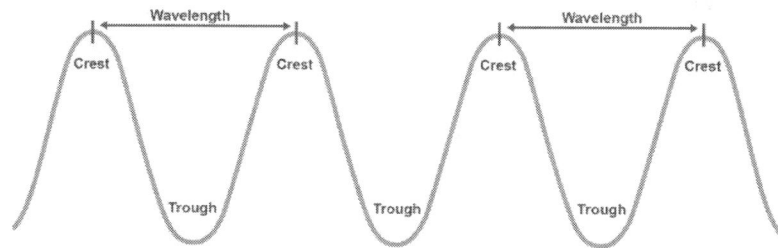

In any organization, the lifeblood of the business are new business leads at the top of the sales funnel that the organization can then turn into real opportunities that generate revenue. As a sales person, I was always haunted by building a pipeline and then draining the pipeline. A pipeline can be defined as all the opportunities you are chasing that may lead to real revenue for the company. In the graphic above, the top crest is a robust pipeline. As one works these deals, either winning or losing them, and does not replace them, one eventually gets to the trough where they have no new opportunities to work. I developed a close friendship with a

salesperson in the Lawson office who focused on a different industry so we were not in competition with one another. One Friday evening, we started brainstorming on what we could do to lessen the depths of our troughs in the generation of quality leads. The Big Dawg contest was born.

We created a list of valuable "non-selling" activities such as keeping up with people, giving somebody something of business value, attending networking meetings, etc. We would also write something of interest about the software we were selling – what problems it solved, what those solutions looked like, where the value was actually created in the process, and so forth. We assigned a point system to each activity and kept a running total for a week, a month, and a quarter. We operated on the honor system and on a weekly basis one of us would win and the other guy would buy a lunch, a round of golf, or a hat or shirt from our local Big Dog store at the mall. Our slogan was, "If you want to run with the big dawgs, you have to get off the porch." The idea was simple. If you are always in the market creating value for friends or trading beans (more of that to follow), you soon get to know every company or executive who has a need for the types of solutions we offered at Lawson. The two of us quickly became the top sales guys in the office and had a ball with the banter and fun. We simply made a habit of doing things that created value for others and held each other accountable.

Years later, I was asked to come work for a local consultancy, Tactica Technology Group, and build an Oracle implementation practice. You may recall that 10 years earlier a friend and I had met when I was at Andersen Consulting and discussed starting a company together. Flash forward and I now have a clue on how to sell enterprise solutions. I also understand how to implement these solutions, so his request to help with building an Oracle implementation practice was something I knew a fair amount about. I joined Tactica in 2001 and soon after, it was sold to Hitachi Consulting. In 2003, my friend and I got serious about starting our own consulting firm. Once again, I would be responsible for sales and marketing. What I learned in my time at Lawson, and with the Big Dawg contest, was that networking and sales could be and needed to be taught to consultants. The other benefit was that I had already created much of the methodology that we could leverage at our new company, which we named Pariveda Solutions. Hitachi Consulting had a direct sales force, and I suggested that we start a company that did not have sales people. Rather, we would teach this methodology to everyone in the company, and we would *all* be responsible for business development.

I quit my job in June of 2003 to launch Pariveda Solutions, Inc. My partner joined me in October of that year and we set off to build a different kind of consulting firm. We morphed what I had built into a concept called *Networking for Life* and it became part of every

employee's training and part of the company's individual review process for all consultants. When I decided after nine years to leave Pariveda in 2012, the company had grown to well over 250 employees without a single direct sales person. In 2016, as of this writing, I have heard from those in the marketplace that Pariveda's growth rate continues and they are still leveraging many of these ideas.

Connect for Life takes what I created at Lawson and goes further than networking. It is about building trusted networks of people in your life and helping those people become successful. Connecting should be the goal for all the relationships in our lives, not just in sales or other business endeavors. Why? Because connecting with others in an authentic way creates value for everyone involved. For my grandfather, connecting was essential to his becoming an executive who invested in a company that launched a new, radical technology (frozen foods), and in working to give back to society in his role as a chemist for UNICEF. When I reflect on my father building a business in a horrible economy, he was able to do it through a number of trusted relationships and relentless pursuit. As I reflect on my career and success, I can't remember a decision that I've made or a need that I've had in the last 30 years that didn't start with a call or an email to somebody in my network. In fact, if you review the friends I've mentioned in my stories, most are still very good friends whom I love and respect. We share mutual appreciation, fill

in for a weakness of one with a strength existing in the other, and we mentor and coach each other. These are good friends and great advisors, who have richly blessed and helped me become the best I could be. There is no way, in the tough times outlined above, that I could have made it without the help of others. The individuals mentioned here are only the short list of people in my life who were part of my success, and in many cases served as my safety net.

This book is aimed at assisting the knowledge worker who has never been taught that the real value we create is outside of the solutions provided. It is about relationships, and the passing on of the "how to" of doing the work; then exposing tools and techniques from networking to selling that will propel one's career. It also focuses on the entrepreneur in technology or the consulting industry who has the desire and drive to start their own company.

We live in an exciting time of technical innovation, but the truth is that there is a wide gap between high-quality technology consultants and those who wear the title but cannot provide the best solutions to their clients. Companies need trusted sources for those technical individuals, so they typically pick a brand in the marketplace. However, if you look at where innovation and technology is taking us, we live in a time of sharing and connecting. What companies need is a trusted advisor who can lead them through the jungle of tech speak and complicated jargon. That

trusted advisor no longer needs to work for the "brand" company if he or she is able to bring quality talent to a company because of his or her relationships.

When I talk about a "brand" company like Pariveda or one of their counterparts of sufficient size, I mean that they have enough critical mass and experience in various marketplaces and have developed executive trust. For a startup qualified in the craft, one can still deliver the same type of value as a branded company through the relationships developed and maintained. Remember, your customer trusts you. If one makes a recommendation or brings an independent consultant on board, the client will trust that you will make sure that the project succeeds.

Because we are an increasingly networked economy, the premium value is on developing a trusted network and deploying those resources to your customers without your having to directly employ those resources. This becomes valuable as technology companies have a tough time keeping their star employees since these employees often branch out into small groups of independent consultants specializing in some type of solution set. Imagine how powerful it would be if you could be the conduit for connecting the talent of these smaller teams to clients who have specific needs? As an independent consultant, one still needs connections at the brand companies because projects will inevitably be proposed that are of sufficient scale to require an introduction to the

trusted people at the branded company. As a larger brand company, what if all your employees took responsibility for selling and were regularly in the marketplace connecting with others? How could you lose? It all comes back to competence, trust, and a solid network.

This book is primarily targeted at the service economy surrounding technology or technical solutions for companies in the business-to-business (B2B) world. It is meant to enable technical individuals to make and keep trusted relationships and then leverage those relationships to deliver value in the marketplace without a direct salesforce. However, if you are a seller of technical and complex solutions, this book will streamline your learning. If you are a technologist, it will open your eyes to things you have never been taught. Technologists, engineers, accountants, and lawyers tend to be more introverted by nature. So while they have a depth of expertise, they are less likely to engage in what is commonly known as networking. You know the event. You show up after work to a big room and exchange cards with others so you can go home with a pile of cards. I'm talking about something entirely different.

HOW TO USE THIS BOOK

This book is divided into two sections. Part One focuses on the reasons for connecting, and why givers of their time and talent progress in their

careers and live better than takers. You will not only learn why it is important to connect, but you will also learn skills to help you build and maintain a network. Even back in the day before blogging, it was important to write relevant content about interesting topics that were pertinent to a set of people struggling for answers. I spent a considerable amount of time while at Pariveda Solutions going to college campuses and encouraging students to learn how to build and nurture their networks. Connecting the concept of "it's not what you know, it's who you know" with the notion of creating knowledge capital implies that it *does matter* what you know and is a lesson that many have parlayed into success in information technology (IT) consulting. *Connecting for Life* is about trusting in the idea that the more you give, the more you get in return.

This book explains the difference between the act of networking and the depth of connecting. It also offers a very useful system that will assist in keeping track of your progress. Think of networking as the actions we carry out in the marketplace – the *what you do* activities. Think of connecting as the result of a deeper level of association in the relationship. In the blockbuster movie *Avatar* the two main characters who fall in love utter a phrase that has multiple layers to it: "I see you." Literally the phrase *to see* means to observe, but is that all the characters mean by this statement? No, they are talking about a deeper

sense of seeing, as in "I see into you. I feel you. I am you." Transitioning to true connectedness is the migration from the activities of networking to forming a deeper relationship. You want to reach a point in your network where the people with whom you have built relationships know they can count on you because actively try to help them.

Connect for Life will lead you through an exercise of deciding what activities you think are important to track for your skill set, and then you will learn how you can integrate these activities into the Touchpoints software that we offer as a helpful tool for connecting. Touchpoints is the tool created to transition the knowledge you have learned in this book and concentrate that insight toward action. The application helps you track your activities and creates a visual status on how you are doing based on the criteria you have set for yourself. A generated heat map of your most effective activities and the results that they create reinforces the key activities you are engaged in and enables you to move forward. Much like the electronic fitness trackers or the multitude of other individual progress measuring tools on the market, Touchpoints is your personal coach to reinforce your daily activities.

On a broader level, the book covers motivations, techniques, and the difference between being connected online through social media, and truly being connected. It is really designed for anyone who wants to improve his or her life beyond networking. Whether you are a college

student, a consultant, a lawyer, or a businessperson in a big or small company, connecting with people is the key skill. As previously described, the goal is to migrate from an action verb, networking, to a truly connected relationship where trust is shared between individuals. We live in a world where everyone is connected through social media such as LinkedIn, Facebook, SnapChat, Twitter, or other social media applications. The notion is that because we are taking part in the community, we are connected. But are we really connected? I would contend that these connections are the beginning of the relationship, or in many cases the rekindling of an older relationship. Finding people online is one of the great rewards of social media, but we also need to further our efforts to progress this transition to trust. Social media connections are not relationships based on trust; they are an act of networking. I am not discounting the need for social networking, as it is vitally important to start or reinvigorate a relationship. However, developing trust is critical. In order to connect for life, one must build networks and connections of trusted individuals whom they can rely on for something, such as quality work, a good tune-up, a well-trimmed lawn, a new car, or a new prospect or client. Because we live in an increasingly shared, mobile, and interconnected economy, connecting for life is more important than ever, especially for the technical solution provider. When there is mutual trust between people then both benefit

from the relationship. One may have a particularly challenging problem at some point and need the expertise of the other, then later the roles may be reversed. In a relationship people can count on each other to help when needed. That is the magic of truly connecting.

Part Two of this book will transition from external networking and connecting to explore navigating within a company or selling to a company. Most technology services companies establish projects in large enterprises. If all that is accomplished by the end of the project is delivery of the work and moving on to the next project or client, then you have missed connecting for life on the inside of the enterprise. It is difficult to navigate most companies. I would contend that any business with more than 100 people is complex. Because of this complexity, it is not always obvious what the formal or informal decision structures are and how things get done. The first question to ask is, "Why is it complex?" The obvious answer is because human beings are involved, and we are by definition, complex. Our relationships are complex. The politics that exist in almost every company build over time, and the only way one can break through and understand them is to build a web of connections and learn some techniques on how to navigate the enterprise.

Inter-enterprise networking and connecting is crucial to success in business and is an important, yet often overlooked dynamic. As a

leader in a consulting firm, I regularly instructed my managers to supervise by walking around. If this is carried out, the conversation inside the company starts and ends with a discussion of the human dynamic. I encourage managers to deliver bad news to executives prior to status meetings as this leads to effective account control. Never surprise executives in a status meeting. I heard a funny statement once that went like this: "Bad news goes around the world four times before good news gets out the front door." Understanding how to navigate this complexity requires an understanding of both connecting and sales, navigating and posturing, isolating and overcoming. The key to success is to use the knowledge you have about an organization, and parlay that knowledge into delivering quality solutions for the client. Sometimes, companies are their own worst enemies because change can bring out the worst in people. One has to be the person who navigates the politics and delivers more value than clients expect.

This is the reason we need to bring to light various principles leveraged by successful sales people and create the linkage between networking and selling that leads to winning and delivering value. In my career, I learned to speak the truth and put the customer first, and then deliver value before I was ever responsible for keeping a group of consultants busy and billable. At Lawson, and later at Hitachi and Pariveda, I became a student of sales and devoured many of the major

books written on selling. Adopting a hybrid of connecting and selling techniques have served me well throughout my career. This book assembles the highlights from tried-and true techniques used the world over.

Notably, there are two types of sales people – the naturals who are successful but can't really tell you "how" they do it; and the process people who methodically apply themselves to the profession of selling. While the "natural" can sharpen the saw by reading this text, the neophyte of sales can learn how to become a sales leader. In the context of this book selling is not about your personality makeup. It is about bringing valuable solutions to the right people in the organization so they can make the best decision for the enterprise. It is also about gaining access as a trusted advisor so one can determine what the obstacles are in the first place. This is not a book on slick techniques, rather, it is about learning to cultivate good solutions delivered at the right value proposition to one's customer. If you can't deliver that value, you should find another prospect. If you can learn to solve real problems with finesse and tact, in an authentic and caring-for-the-customer fashion, you will be providing a service that few deliver.

If you apply yourself and are out there being a giving and helpful person, the phone will ring, a text or an email will come in, or someone will contact you on social media. The preliminary hard work is giving your

life away through connecting. Learning the sales techniques and process will allow you to combine your networking prowess with effective ways to deliver value for customers. *Connect for Life* is NOT traditional networking. It is about building and creating trusted relationships by delivering knowledge and ideas which can be exchanged in confidence. That circle of trust expands geometrically as you build touch points. While the knowledge worker (what we will call the target audience) knows a plethora about their domain, they may not know the best way to get that message out into the market. Connecting does just that, but in an un-networking way. All things being equal, people would rather buy from those they know and trust.

By focusing on teaching basic sales processes and techniques, a knowledge worker can become more successful because they understand the solution part of the equation. Articulating the solution and wrapping that solution in some process, will improve the probability of success. Consider how most knowledge workers sell their ideas inside of an enterprise. They create the idea and then vet that idea in a trusted and closed environment. Next, as the idea develops throughout the organization, they gain sponsorship for the idea. Often, an executive who likes a specific idea becomes the voice or navigator for that idea inside the company. The knowledge worker may not realize that he has migrated from innovator, to sales person, to sales support, but this is

what has happened. Every aspect of moving an idea through each gate of the process inside of the enterprise is a miniature sale. In the movie *Apollo 13*, three astronauts encountered catastrophic failure that changed the planned outcome of their space journey from a walk on the moon, to returning to earth safely. In all of the tension and drama, it is easy to lose track of the little sales cycles that were transpiring at NASA as various engineers were pitching their ideas to save the lives of the three astronauts. Idea after idea was discussed in small groups, then in larger groups, and finally the decision-making group. At each step of the way, the best ideas were backed up by the best evidence that a particular solution was the best, or not. Beneath the surface of these deliberations were relationships and trust, established by months and years of working together. It is what allowed various individuals to present their ideas and for others to listen. The process allowed a contrarian idea to change the way key individuals were analyzing the best solution. The movie was a great example of technical enterprise sales that led to the best set of outcomes one after another to bring three men back to Earth alive. The flight control leader, Gene Kranz, said it best: "This crisis was NASA's finest hour."

By creating the mindset of a problem solver, you will become a connector and a leader in your organization. What if your organization could be successful without sales people? What if the individuals with the

domain knowledge actually solved the complex problems of their customers without external resources? What if our knowledge worker is well connected, well respected as a giver, and has learned basics sales skills? What if every member of an implementation team managed by walking around inside the client site learning more about who the client is and what their challenges are? Could that be a competitive advantage? Many companies operate this way, and they are very successful. But they do so deliberately and with a focus on developing people.

Whether connecting in the marketplace to help others or finding the right person or company to solve your problem, connectors create real value for themselves and the organizations they work with. I remember a vice president of a consulting firm who did business for a large retail energy provider really exemplifying this skill. He was so adept at understanding the internal politics, the personality differences between executives, and the nuances of the business that the energy provider used him as a conduit to make change. He became the communication vehicle between executives and departments, the glue that helped a very fast-growing company cope with rapid change. Along the way, he was privy to the real challenges of the business for which his consulting firm was uniquely qualified to create solutions. By connecting, learning, and giving he was able to sell project after project and delivered $10 million in services over a three-year period. This is a wonderful example of

merging connecting externally and internally together while using sales techniques to ensure a message was getting to the right decision makers. This also showed the importance of having emotional intelligence, rather than pure IQ horsepower. Emotional intelligence allows you to sense, feel, and empathize with your client in ways that IQ sometimes misses. If you think this is a challenge for you, partner with others in selling and connecting who have that skill and learn the triggers. It will be time well spent.

In my career, I have been able to create success whether selling enterprise solutions to large firms or starting a consulting firm and expanding it without a dedicated sales force. The most rewarding aspect of teaching these methods has been watching individuals become more self-determined and independent. I have observed many who were under my training go on to achieve great success and in many cases launch entrepreneurial ventures on their own. I think that the best measurement of success is to consider how many others you have helped.

The secret sauce is a recipe of connecting, selling, and having a road map that will lead you to success. If you trust and follow the *Connect for Life* process, you will be rewarded both personally and professionally.

Good luck connecting! - John

PART ONE - Building Connections

As you begin your journey, focus on casting a wide net and being authentic in all that you do. By just being nice and helpful, you will be amazed at what can happen. You will learn that by being a giver, the natural laws of reciprocity activate. The age-old saying, "What goes around, comes around," will never be truer in any other activity than it is in connecting. The more you give, the more you connect, and the more it comes back to you in ways you can never know or predict. The friends and relationships you form will change your life and be in your life forever.

By genuinely giving, you will begin to see that business is about choosing to be surrounded by those whom you trust and admire. I promise that if you apply yourself to these practices, you will never go hungry, never want for a dollar, and no organization will ever control your future. You will be able to live by the tenet that you received ten times more than you were ever able to give away to others. Best of all, you will enjoy your work life, your home life, and your relationships more than ever.

Chapter 1 - Why Connect at All?

People can spend their entire career trying to answer the question "Why?" across a wide range of topics: Why do we work so hard? Why are people mean? Why am I being held back from being successful? I don't know on the psychological level why we ask why, but for me it is simple. Connecting represents a shorter distance between two points, and I want to get to point B as quickly as possible. I could do things the hard way or the easy way. On some level, I guess that thinking this way makes me a taker because I originally wanted to connect so that I could win at business and life. I figured the more people I knew and who knew me, the better I would be able to meet my goals. I never really dug that deep in my heart because where I ended up seemed like a good place, and those around me view me as a helper. A recent example of this was my experience in refinancing my house. I was shopping online one Saturday and saw that I could take my mortgage rate from 4.25% to 3% and the term from 30 years to 15 years and keep my payments roughly the same. I was approved in about 15 minutes, but the process of underwriting the new loan was a nightmare. Request after request came in with the underwriter asking me for just a little bit more information. Interaction with an online website asking me for more and more information was making me crazy, mostly because it took a lot of time;

and partly because I was in the business of building customer applications like this portal to "make things easier for the client." Whoa! I almost quit the process three times telling myself that the savings I would receive was not worth the time and aggravation. After three months and as the closing was postponed for the third time, I had had enough. I got on the company's website and found the top three executives. I figured out what their email addresses were and I sent them all a nice but firm note about how challenging this process was, and that I was hoping somebody at the executive level would call me. Since I have served on many boards and run a few businesses, I have seen many nasty emails where people vent and then fire off a missile. I thought, even though I'm frustrated, if this was my business, I'd want to know, so I wrote a very informative email with no visceral intent.

The next morning, I got a call from the chief operating officer as I was on the way to the airport. She was very open to listening and asked several questions about how they might improve their services. Because of my background in consulting I threw out a few ideas. Then we started talking in general about my overall client experience, and I told her about a consulting firm that I had used at my current company. I thought the company was very good and might be able to help them take a quick look at their issue. I told her our challenge and how they had helped us. She asked me if I would make an introduction and also if I would talk to

her product manager to provide some context and feedback about my experience with the online portal. I made an introduction with someone at the company I had recommended, and I scheduled time to talk with the product manager a few days later. She was very appreciative and was also able to review my loan and determine why I had slipped through the cracks. By the time I got home from a three-day business trip, I had the closing scheduled, but more importantly, I had helped some people who really cared about their company and the service they provided. I don't know if I will ever hear from the company again, or whether it will ever lead to a dime of income but it doesn't matter. I was a customer with expertise in an area they needed, and the chief operating officer of the company was willing to listen and take action. I had a great week of travel and customer meetings, but this was the most rewarding thing I had accomplished the entire week. And this is how it works. Give yourself away and you will make great friends and will never go hungry.

In his book, *Taming Your Gremlin*, Rick Carson describes the life we have as a view out of our wonderful covering of skin. We can see the world as we want to see it, but most of us are fighting a battle against a gremlin in our thought-life who is trying to take us down. The root of the gremlin's banter inside of our head is over the question, "Why?" Not why in regard to the meaning of life, but why did this or that happen, and what does it mean to you today. Sometimes we wear ourselves out with these

questions when we are hurt, or when bad things happen, or when we feel inadequate. As Carson points out in the book, the gist of trying to answer the, "Why?" question is largely a waste of time. Often the people and circumstances are not there to provide an answer, nor will they ever be. In Carson's book, the gremlin is that voice in our head that creates fear, uncertainty, and doubt in our circumstances. These three things, which Carson refers to as FUD, are what keep us all from achieving our potential. If you are having doubts about your ability to be the very best you can be and are doubting your ability to accomplish what is written in this book, you need to explore what is holding you back. Is it fear, uncertainty, or doubt? Do you feel inadequate, or just plain shy? Reading *Taming your Gremlin* will help you overcome those fears and silence the voice in your head that is telling you that you are not good enough. The reason I bring up this topic is because I have witnessed people to whom I was teaching my methodology freeze even though they were fantastic at their jobs. Often, these were the people who were sought out as experts or those who could be relied upon. Because of fear, they limited their potential and struggled with connecting and networking with others. The saying goes, "People don't change until the pain to stay the same is greater than the pain to change." That may be true but if you trust me on this, you can put all of the naysayers to bed when you achieve greatness by giving of yourself and connecting with others.

Life is a funny thing. The advantage of being a little older is that you see things differently in the rearview mirror. In the movie *Sahara*, the star Matthew McConaughey has a line, "Every great thing that's ever happened to me happened in the water." When I think about my life, every good thing that has ever happened to me happened as a result of a relationship or connection. As I chronicle my life, looking at the college I picked, the friends I have, the woman I married, the schools my kids attended, the profession I chose – it all happened because of relationships and connections. It might not have been a first-level relationship as defined by LinkedIn with a response to "I'd like to connect with you," but it was an introduction, a name, a phone number, a piece of advice – always connected to a person I trusted.

When I review my career, the only resume I used to get a job was my first one. I doubt that I would have made it in a world where college students have internships every summer and then somewhere along the way, before the beginning of their senior year, they have a job offer in hand. I was feeling proud of myself with my double major and only six hours to take in my last semester in college and was a little late to the game. I wrote and re-wrote my resume and signed up for an interview at Texas American Bank in Fort Worth, as they were coming for on campus interviews. The interview went well, and I got a job offer. I've filled out resumes since then as a request from writers or for graduate

school, but never to get a job. Ever since that first job I obtained employment because someone took an interest in me or because I struck up a relationship with someone and we talked about mutual interests. Most of the time the interaction started with a kind word, a warm introduction to a like-minded person, or a problem solved over a cup of coffee.

It just makes sense, doesn't it? As humans we are designed to be in and around people. People are the mission, not the things we accumulate in life. I always tell my children and those who worked for me, "Find something you love to do with people you love to be around and it will never seem like work. The money will just show up." I also found it is easier to connect with people to get a job done. You can't possibly know everything yourself, and if you surround yourself with people who have more skill than you, you will succeed. As Harvey Mackay states in his book *How to Dig Your Well Before You're Thirsty,* "You transfer the strength of an individual to the strength of a group." If you have ever been in one of those large tug of war games with 20 or 30 people, you know what he means. It is difficult to see the impact of a single individual in the process of winning or losing, but when the entire group is pulling in the same direction, everyone wins. There is a great networking group in Dallas that I helped to create in 2003 when I started Pariveda. The DFW IT Round Table is a group of like-minded leaders

from various types of technology firms. The group has met twice a month since 2003 and starts with three things – wins, needs, and thank-yous. The majority of the thank-yous are aimed toward other members who helped an individual with a lead, a proposal, a job change, or anything that a member needed. I have pitched business plans and asked individuals to review specific things that I was trying to accomplish. The group was always helpful and improved my ideas. That led me to coaching others and helping them with critical negotiations, new job opportunities, or entirely new business ideas. Everyone in that group is committed to giving and helping others within the group. It is truly a special thing and a living metaphor to the ideas in this book. Life is too short and too hard to go through it alone. If you focus on being a true connector, you can be happier and accomplish more than you could ever imagine.

The other thing you need to realize is that people want to help you. In his book, *The Power of Who: You Already Know Everyone You Need to Know,* Bob Beaudine says traditional networking has changed because you already have a group of people who want to help you with whatever you need. His argument is that for all of the networking he has done, it is a small group of people who actually helped him in his career. In taking that idea to the next level, being a connector for yourself and for others creates more value for all of those people in your network.

Chapter 2 - Givers and Takers

The secret of success is not a secret. Most of the successful people in the world tend to write down what they did to become successful. As I gaze across my bookshelves I see books by Buffet, Rockefeller, Carnegie, and lesser-known names such as Peter Thiel (founder of PayPal), Jim Cramer (founder of Mad Money), and Harvey Mackey (renowned speaker and author of many books on sales and relationships). They all share a very similar trait, the ability to share their success through stories. Later in the book we will discuss stories in great length, but if you go back in history prior to the printing press, the families, tribes, and societal culture used stories to pass the lore from generation to generation. Instead of just saying someone is brave, the people would tell a very detailed story about what that person did to be known as being brave.

I remember a case where I was working on a seven-figure software deal for about a year. Just days before I was going to fly out to the corporate headquarters of the company, the CIO quit, and I got a call that the deal was off. I simply said, "Well, I was headed to the airport anyway and we have all worked too hard to have this conversation over the phone, so I'll be there this afternoon." With that, I stood up from the sales meeting I was attending, asked my assistant to book a flight and a

hotel in that small town. I called my wife and told her I would not be home for dinner. After landing, I drove two hours to the company where I discussed with the executives the risks of doing nothing. I reminded them of the reasons why they wanted to do it in the first place, particularly relating to the problems they had with their payroll system. I asked, "Why don't I stick around for a few days, and we'll work through something that will work for you? They agreed. By the end of the week, I was calling my boss in Chicago to tell him that I had a signed six-figure contract and had received a check for 50% of the contract amount.

That story became lore at the software company where I worked. As one reads those words, one may identify with my struggles and challenges. Everyone who has ever sold for a living has had things blow up without warning. It's one thing to say never give up. It is another thing entirely to tell people a story on how perseverance and determination can lead to success.

So many of the top business people whose books line my office shelves share another characteristic, they are givers. Warren Buffet is so transparent that annually shareholders of Berkshire Hathaway flock to Omaha to hear Buffet and his partner, Charlie Munger, tell their stories about various businesses or their perspective on the economy. They are known for being straight shooters. People are not only attracted to the success that Berkshire Hathaway has created for its shareholders, but

also the company's Midwest frankness. Their giving comes in the form of advice and perspective. In a world of spin doctors and politicians doing what the last survey said to do, directness is refreshing. The world needs more direct and candid discourse. One may not be able to duplicate what Buffet has done for his shareholders, but how he has gone about it is not a secret. The successful people I meet often want to share their trials and tribulations, successes and failures. That is, unless they are takers. Takers view the world as a zero-sum game where in order for them to win, you must lose.

The Rockefellers are also givers but in a different way. According to the National Park Service website:

The Rockefeller family's efforts to protect the Grand Tetons began shortly after John D. Rockefeller, Jr. was invited in 1926 to visit the area by Horace Albright, then superintendent of the nearby Yellowstone National Park and later Director of the National Park Service. During his visit, Rockefeller became concerned that increasing growth and commercialism of the valley would threaten its future.

Although the idea of protecting the Tetons began as early as the 1880s, there was little support in Congress and by local ranchers who felt government involvement would reduce their personal freedoms, limit cattle grazing rights and drain

Teton County's tax base. Throughout the 1920s, however, many reluctantly agreed that the remote area and glacial lakes were not conducive to farming and grazing, and could be protected. But there was no agreement about the Snake River valley floor. Albright and others feared the land would be purchased by developers and turned into something of an amusement park.

Responding to this concern, Rockefeller established a blind trust, and in the 1920s spent $1.5 million secretly buying ranches in the valley that were for sale through the Snake River Company with the intention of turning them over to the National Park Service.

President Franklin Roosevelt created the Jackson Hole National Monument in 1943. The federally protected area incorporated national forests, various public and private lands. In 1949, Rockefeller donated 33,000 acres to the National Park Service, which became the heart of the park. The following year, President Harry Truman merged the two areas and established Grand Teton National Park.

Part of the gift included a state-of-the-art, 7,500 square-foot preserve center on the property. The structure is the first platinum-level Leadership in Energy and Environmental Design (LEED) certified building to be built in the National Park System.

The Laurance S. Rockefeller Preserve Center, with an eight-mile network of trails to scenic and ecologically significant areas of the preserve, including Lake Creek, Phelps Lake and the adjacent ridges, opened to the public in June 2008.

Why They Gave

The Rockefeller family has a long tradition of supporting national parks through philanthropy. They've established or enhanced more than 20 national parks from Maine to Wyoming including: Grand Teton, Acadia, Virgin Islands, Shenandoah, and Great Smoky Mountains. As an advisor to five American presidents and chairman of the Outdoor Recreation Resource Review Commission and President's Advisory Council, Laurance S. Rockefeller, son of John D. Rockefeller Jr., helped place conservation issues on the national agenda.

"I have always shared my father's vision, not only to give generously but also that people should live in harmony with nature," Rockefeller said through a spokesman before the presentation ceremony of the ranch in 2001. "For 75 years, the majestic property has been preserved for our family, and I am gratified that henceforth it will be preserved for the American people."

When you visit this area, you are struck by the majesty and beauty that will be a gift to Americans for centuries to come.

In his book, *Give and Take*, Adam Grant, Ph.D., lays the foundation for pondering the concept "why givers do better in almost every way." The author lays out study after study and example after example of successful individuals who care more about helping others than they do gathering mantles of success for themselves.

Early in the book, Grant uses several examples to compare and contrast givers and takers. One illustration in the book is of Kenneth Lay, former Chairman of Enron. Grant describes Lay as a faux "giver". Grant contends that Lay was really looking out for his own best interests above all others, which ultimately caused the Houston company's failure; indicative of a real taker. From the size of his full-page portrait in Enron's annual report, to the use of company assets for personal gain, Lay took and took until it destroyed the company. In one example, it is documented that $4.5 million in travel commissions went to a travel agency owned by Lay's sister. As further proof, right before Enron went under, Lay sold $70 million worth of stock. The investigations that followed revealed fraud, abuse, and self-absorption of the highest degree.

In contrast, Grant talks about the successful billionaire, Jon Huntsman, who lived his entire life as a contributor. For those who don't

know of Jon Huntsman, he is an outstanding businessman and politician. His father founded the Huntsman Container Corporation, which is famous for creating the clamshell box for the McDonald's Big Mac. The younger Huntsman became very successful in his own right and established Huntsman Chemical among other companies. Along the way, he served as Governor of Utah from 2005 to 2009. In 2008 he won reelection by 78%, and in 2009 he was selected to be the United States Ambassador to China. In 2012 he resigned as ambassador to seek the Republican nomination for President. Huntsman gave generously throughout his career, but he is also known for not taking the last dollar in a negotiation. In one story relayed by Grant, Huntsman was negotiating a multi-hundred-million-dollar divestiture while the wife of the CEO he was negotiating against was dying of an illness. While Huntsman knew there was still more that he could get in the negotiation, he decided that he didn't want to expose the opposing CEO to greater stress, so Huntsman ceased negotiations and finalized the deal. Moreover, there is a story where Huntsman made a handshake deal with a divisional president for this individual to purchase a portion of one of the companies for something in the mid-fifty-million-dollar range. Over the next six months while they worked out the details, the market turned positive and the division grew in value to $250 million. Even the buyer went back to Huntsman and offered to split the difference because it was

inequitable to Huntsman. Huntsman refused and declared, "A deal's a deal."

It would seem that integrity and giving are connected although Grant doesn't delve too deeply into that topic. What is evident in the data is that givers are typically more successful and lead fuller lives.

In his timeless book, *How to Win Friends and Influence People*, Dale Carnegie outlines six basic tenets that all givers should live by. Everyone would benefit by reading this book each year to absorb its simplicity. It is fascinating to ruminate that this advice was conveyed to the world in 1936. A few examples of topics from the book are:

- Fundamental Techniques in Handling People

- Six Ways to Make People Like You

- Win People to Your Way of Thinking

- Be a Leader: How to Change People Without Giving Offense or Arousing Resentment

The prescription is timeless and simple. Whether encouraging us to simply smile or to recall that the sweetest sound to anyone's ear is the sound of his or her own name, Carnegie's instruction is abiding for all generations. Carnegie chronicles his options from the other person's perspective, and his advice applies even more so today. In fact, the book has sold over 30-million copies worldwide, has been translated into multiple languages, and in 2011 was put on the list of the top 100 most

influential books of all time. Givers treat everyone with respect and work

on ways to help and encourage others and this advice from Mr. Carnegie

shows us how.

Chapter 3 - Networking for Life

So here you are, at the precipice. You have heard of this concept of networking and you have bought into the idea that it works. You genuinely like to help people and would consider yourself a giver, but now you must begin the process. You may already be on social media sites and exchanging thoughts and ideas with others. Is that networking? What else should you be doing? The purpose of this section is to expand your skills in growing your network. By becoming an effective networker and building an effectual network, you will be successful in sales, and will be prepared for success in life. Moving from networking to connecting is a journey and a process, but first things first.

The Network Effect

A network is a dynamic set of relationships that grow exponentially as you increase numbers. The Network Effect is the concept that the value of a network increases as more connections are made to the network. Bob Metcalfe developed this concept in 1973. Mr. Metcalfe founded a company named 3Com; the company that invented the modern-day Ethernet network. Metcalfe had the idea that you could connect users in a company through basic cabling. Simply by being connected, extended value would be created for the company because users would be able to exchange information and documents collaboratively. Mr. Metcalfe is

credited with saying that the value of a network, "is proportional to the square of the number of connected users." This is the math behind the definition of the "network effect." Imagine, before the Internet, social media, and smart phones this simple concept changed the world and was the genesis of the concept of networking. By connecting people through machines, individuals could create greater value by collaborating. The technical infrastructure definition of a network is a combination of hardware and software that routes packets of information between participants.

Today we have email, social media, and smart phones. We are electronically connected across the world in real time and take Metcalf's metaphor to an entirely new level. But do we? We may be connected but somewhere along the way, we forgot to personalize the connection. Unlocking that value to the connection *is* the secret.

It starts with building a network that will grow exponentially in value the more you feed and nurture it. The following graphic illustrates how interconnected nodes in a network can expand exponentially.

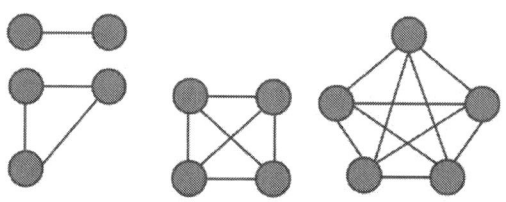

# of People	# of potential matches
2	1
3	3
4	6
5	10
6	15

Source: Ford harding, Making Rainmakers, 2006

According to Harvey Mackay, author of *Dig Your Well Before You're Thirsty,* a network is an investment that you should invest your life in developing. I heard him say that if his building was on fire, he'd grab his folder of contacts and relationships and head for the door. In the old days, contacts were kept in a Rolodex, a collection of business cards, names, and numbers on a plastic wheel. When people got fancy, they put business cards in sleeves in a notebook and arranged them alphabetically. Today, contacts live on your phone and travel with you everywhere you go.

According to Mr. Mackay, everything is replaceable *except* relationships. He outlines several factors about what a network can do for you.

- A network replaces the weakness of the individual with the strength of a group.

- A network can review that big report or give you advice on your pitch.

- My network can help you expand your network.

- A network can enrich your life anywhere in the world.

- A network can provide you with new experiences and knowledge.

- Networking can help you help others.

- Job security? Don't rely on the corporation. Rely on your network.

- A network can make you look good but freshen each contact every six months.

- A network expands your financial reach infinitely.

As you consider the information in this book, remember that you are not just a consumer of this material, but will eventually become a teacher. Success in networking will lead to success in connecting. You will become recognized for that success, and others will ask for help. It is up to you to pass it on. They say if you can teach it, you know it.

Where Do I Start?

It's like the question, "How do you eat an elephant?" The answer is, "one bite at a time." Every journey begins with the first step. Hopefully, this book provides you with a roadmap and guides you from step to step. You may be starting this process having spent a career connecting or networking, and you would like to sharpen the saw. Or perhaps you have never been exposed to connecting in this way. Perhaps you are a college student, and you know intellectually that you should develop a network while in college. It doesn't matter why or where you are in the process. The key is to start with the first step from where you are, not where you think you should be.

To the student of connecting, think about this chapter as training camp. Throughout our careers, we often move away from the fundamentals of a particular skill that brought us success earlier in life. Networking is one of those activities. As a big sports fan, I'm always excited when football season is around the corner. I have watched college and professional athletes prepare for training camp. The players all hate camp, but they know it sets the tone for the rest of the season. You'd better show up well-conditioned or you won't make it through the two or three practices a day. At the start of camp, it is always back to the basics of the sport. The game of football has become enormously more complicated. Athletes must not only be physically sound but also

intellectually sharp. At the professional level, there are no more dumb jocks playing the game. Even the pros, on day one, are running, throwing, blocking, and catching the ball. As they go through camp, these athletes go back to things they have been doing since grade school, practicing the basics of their craft.

The famous football coach, Vince Lombardi, was known as a guy who always focused on fundamentals. In his book, *Zigler on Selling,* Zig Zigler begins the book with a story of Lombardi. Under Lombardi, the Green Bay Packers won the first two Super Bowls, Super Bowls I and II. During the season, if the team ever had a bad game, the following week of practice would begin with the basics of their craft. Lombardi would say, "Gentlemen, we performed below the standards we have set for ourselves as a championship football team. This week we are going to return to the fundamentals." Lombardi understood the importance of the fundamentals of his craft.

What are the basics of your craft? Ask yourself, "Am I really doing well in the networking part of my life?" I saw Zig Zigler speak in Dallas one weekend, and a line he used stuck with me. He was reciting the story of Lombardi referenced in his book above and talking about good habits, getting back to basics, and being honest about your performance. He said, "You know, you can fool your boss and you can fool your friends but don't ever try to fool yourself." He added,

"Remember the 11th commandment – thou shall not kid thyself." That thought permeated my mind as I realized that humans are great at rationalizing what we really want to or don't want to do. Rationalizing can be defined as telling ourselves rational lies. Don't do it! Getting back to basics is like drinking cold fresh water; it will propel you to places you never thought you would attain in your life. Plus, you cannot truly connect with others unless you build a habit of networking with them.

I remember in 2003 when the U.S. economy was just coming out of recession. I started working with the DFW IT Round Table, which had great collaboration and participation. It was an inspirational twice-a-month gathering to see peers who shared mutual respect and were actively working on helping each other network. I remember one meeting when I told the group, "It's easy to come here now because the economy is in bad shape. The key for this group will be in our habits to come to these meetings when the economy is good, and we are all flush with business. There will be 10 other things that will feel like they are top priority. Trust me and keep coming." Habits like these will pay dividends your entire life if you remain plugged in.

The List

I often coach people on how to build a network. I start by asking, "Who do you know?" Frequently the answer is, "I don't know anyone." Well,

maybe that is true, but you know more people than you think you know. Use the mind map illustration below, then write down 50 people that fall into the pictured categories.

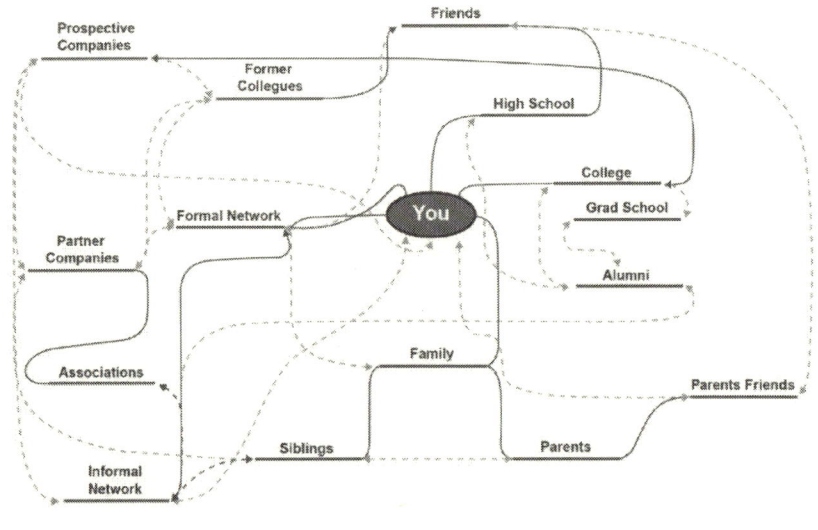

Humphrey - 1999

If you already have this list of folks on LinkedIn or Outlook, pause and log into your account on LinkedIn and ask yourself how often you are in touch with those people or refreshing your network. Author Mackay recommends, "Having a big network is only valuable if you are reaching out and keeping up with people on a regular basis." Mackay also recommends that you add people to your network across a wide range of backgrounds, talents, and skills and then communicate with them every 6 to 12 months. You never know when someone will need to tap your

network to solve a critical problem in their life. Mackay's list starts with these categories of individuals in your personal network.

- Real estate broker
- Source for hard-to-get tickets
- Travel agent
- Catholic/Jewish/Protestant/African American/Feminist community leader, just to name a few
- Headhunter
- Banker
- Elected local official
- High ranking cop
- Firefighters
- Celebrity
- Veterinarian
- Insurance expert
- Divorce lawyer
- Auto mechanic
- Media contact
- Best friend

Let's explore for a moment why you might want some of these people in your network. You might have a need for a source of hard-to-get tickets because on short notice you might have a client coming into town who wants to go to a game. You might connect with a few good headhunters because there is nothing more rewarding than helping someone in need get a job. They will remember it for a long time. You should always have a couple of bankers in mind, not just for yourself, but also for others in your network. Just making a simple connection between someone who wants to loan money and someone who is in the process of looking at financing can pay dividends down the road.

Whether it is a banker introduction, an insurance agent, a lawyer, or simply a good auto mechanic, remember that because somebody trusts you, that introduction can be a solution to another person's problem. Whenever you are the recipient for this type of connection it is critical to follow-up with the connector and not only say thank you but let them know the status. My experience is that people in your network want to help you and a handwritten note and a thank you will go a long way to keeping that connection happy.

Learning how to expand your network and trade beans is critical to your success. Trading beans is the process where you sit with someone in person or on the phone and exchange market intelligence. On the surface it may be about people, technology, ideas, or a specific deal, but beyond that you are sharing information that can enable you both to be more effective. It's not a process where you say, "I'll give you a bean if you give me a bean," but rather two individuals getting together to exchange thoughts and ideas about an idea or transaction. This search for market intelligence will make you smarter than others in the market, and will make your information more valuable. It will also help you to know more about the landscape of your specific target because you will have a greater knowledge concerning the cultures of companies, individual competitors, and what obstacles might need to be addressed, and so forth.

Early in my career of selling technology to companies, I developed a simple spreadsheet of all of the companies I thought fit the targets I needed to go after in my assigned territory. Every week, I would print a copy and bind it in a notebook. Every time I had a bean-trading meeting, I opened up that notebook. Invariably, the individual across the table got wide-eyed and asked something like," What is that?"

I would respond, "This is everything I know about all of these accounts. What do you want to know?" I knew the names of executives-- whether they were a PeopleSoft, JD Edwards, or Oracle shop--what services companies were working there, and any other important fact that I wanted to share. Taking a risk by giving more than I might get always worked in my favor. As other networkers or sales people were grateful, it endeared me to them. For many, we became lifelong friends.

Whether you are selling technology or services doesn't matter, what you are after is leverage. When a larger team is pulling the rope in your direction, leverage occurs. When leverage occurs, you get exponentially more accomplished than you could ever get done by yourself. Your list of contacts needs to be continuously refreshed since acquisitions, divestitures, and closings happen every day and people lose touch and change jobs. You cannot get leverage with outdated or incorrect contacts. Leverage in sales carries an exponential improvement on your probability of success.

Practice, practice, practice

No one has ever purchased tickets to a Broadway show to see the actors

practicing for the first time for an audience. These craftspeople (paid

professionals in their sport) practiced for months memorizing their lines,

blocking their movements on the stage, and learning the lyrics to songs,

over and over, night and day. When the show opens, they are prepared.

So why do we treat our own careers like *hobbies* rather than

performing like professionals? By that I mean, we might have spent more

time studying for a test in college than in preparing for a first meeting

with a new prospect. Sounds crazy, but how many of us have not written

down our rap and practiced it on others? There are a few different types

of settings in which we get to talk about our company or ourselves to

friends, family, our network, a potential employer and/or prospect.

Here are three scenarios that I have developed where I briefly

explain what I do. You should consider creating your own. Remember

what Zigler said about the 11th commandment, "thou shall not kid

thyself." To me, that means write it down and memorize your pitch.

Informal with friends or family

Them: "So what are you doing these days?"

Me: "In 2012, I left the company I had founded in 2003 to pursue

other interests, consult with multiple companies and start

Connect for Life. I'm what is called a serial entrepreneur; which

is another way of saying a guy who grew up with a short attention span and a lot of energy. Helping individuals achieve their highest potential through the relationships they have is the highest form of success."

Specific question from potential client

Them: "Tell me what is unique about Connect for Life?"

Me: "*Connect for Life* is a technology and services company designed to assist people who want to move from networking to connecting; and then learn how to become more effective in both internal and external sales. We currently have a couple of books and a piece of technology that assists the user in tracking his effectiveness or progress around connecting."

More formal at networking event (stand and introduce yourself and company)

Them: "Can you tell us a little bit about you and your firm?"

Me: "Hi, my name is John Humphrey. I founded *Connect for Life,* a relationship and sales driven organization. We are all about helping individuals improve their success both personally and professionally. I look forward to meeting you all and talking further as the evening goes on. Thanks for having me."

I have had so much fun speaking on college campuses concerning this topic. I have always felt richly rewarded whenever I get a call from a former employee or a person I've assisted along their way telling me that they have started their own business or were branching out. It is rewarding when you realize you have something to share and people want the knowledge to improve their lives.

One final word about how we learn and why writing things down is important. I know we all learn differently, but it is a proven fact that when more of a person's five senses are involved in the learning process, the greater the probability of remembering. Something magical happens in the brain when we do this. Write it down. Say it to yourself in front of a mirror. It's almost like your brain takes all of the information that you put in it and when you need them most, the words come out naturally and sometimes in a completely different way than what you originally wrote. This is when you know you have moved from a student of networking to the professional level. When you listen to yourself, the words come out with authority and in your natural speech. Your rap transcends from words on a piece of paper or data in a word processor, to a heartfelt and authentic series of words that make the point you really want to make. Vince Lombardi was also the guy who said, "Practice doesn't make perfect, perfect practice makes perfect." Anything worth doing is worth doing well.

Chapter 4 - Social Media and Social Capital

Before digging into the social media phenomenon, we need to explore what social capital is, and how it can create value for you and those around you. It is generally thought that social capital is the value of all the social networks within a society that allows the society to function properly. Throughout world history many communities would stick together. For instance, members of a community would often stop what they were doing to raise a barn for a neighbor or some other activity that required a team of physical effort. Whether it was sharing the workload or defending a small settlement on the prairie, the concept remains the same. It works akin to an unwritten contract between individuals and communities that has the capability to modify behaviors, enforce rules, and improve the quality of life for everyone within that network. In today's world it would be equivalent to watching over a neighbor's house in their absence for the weekend, or helping a friend move.

However, this concept is evolving. Social capital is morphing online as well. As with every transition, things start out slowly. I believe one reason that social capital is being converted online is because trust is transitioning online as well. To step back and see how things are evolving, just look at our banking system. The first online bank, NetBank, founded in 1996, started out slowly and eventually gained momentum;

and today, you would not even consider a bank that did not have an online platform. We have faith in these systems. Today with banking, finance, retail, audio books, dating sites, just to name a few, we are in an eCommerce society built on trust.

Consider the .com rise of the early 21st Century. Anytime I hear the words "paradigm shift," I duck for cover. Previously, dot-coms were popping up everywhere. Every traditional business was under fire since things had changed. Maybe they had or maybe not. In the rush to gold mines, companies went public with enormous market capitalization rates without revenue or income. Many of them pitched the quality of their connections as a reason to buy their software. The perplexing thing about investing is that you can have the right idea at the wrong time and make an erroneous investment and lose money. If you were an early investor in the "everything changed" phenomenon, and you invested primarily in NASDAQ stocks, you would have lost 75% of your investment when the NASDAQ fell suddenly in 2001. Many of these enterprises did have social capital because they were connecting people in a way that had never been done before; however, it was hard for the markets to figure out who had value (Amazon) or who was a loser (WebVan). When the NASDAQ crashed from the dot-com bubble, suddenly the naysayers won.

Or had they? In the years to follow, some of those companies born in that era created very successful businesses. They had created social capital that created billion-dollar market capitalization rates, some of which are still growing. When you look at the FANG stocks – Facebook, Amazon, Netflix, and Google, you see four companies who not only have been very successful but they are also both innovative and disruptive. They are all network companies that trade at huge multiples to their enterprise value. Many have allowed us to develop social capital. We are able to connect, reconnect, and expand our reach across the globe. We are at the foothills of a long secular trend of connectedness, with the potential downside being that the prospective customer knows more about you and your company *before* you show up for a sales call and you may not have told a good story in your own social media. Our online persona is extremely important and increasingly so. The world will continue to connect at an increasing rate and you must be there engaging in the process or you won't develop your own social capital. Even if you are with a brand company, as described in the introduction, your prospects and customers will seek to know who you are before you make an appearance. If developing social capital is ignored, you are doomed in your ability to add value across a broader scale. There are studies saying that buyers are in control today, much more than sellers. Buyers know who you are because they have read your resume on

LinkedIn and evaluated your network. They know what your company sells and have even vetted your services through their trusted networks. One must not ignore the social capital that is created through social selling.

For the individual, social capital is about the power of that person's connections, relationships, and knowledge. However, it is also about one's personal reputation and story. Because of transparency across a myriad of social media outlets, one needs to protect one's image and reputation to avoid being embarrassed in front of a prospective customer or employer. The purpose of this book is to encourage each one to be a giver and engage in the journey, but it is also a how-to book that provides a roadmap for creating leveraged value for your business life. You will have an enormous amount of social capital if you start giving, building a network, and focusing on connecting in an intimate way.

Being a knowledge worker in today's business community is a boon. For the purposes of this book, I am defining the knowledge worker as someone who is not working in physical labor, but one working with people, processes, and/or technology. This individual is often putting all three of these elements together to solve critical problems for her/his customers with software. The person who understands how these three elements can fit together, and who also understands business, is hugely

valuable in today's economy. There are not enough of these individuals to solve the problems currently facing business today. Even the current immigration debate is slowing the number of foreign nationals who come here to study and then stay. The U.S. could admit every individual who wanted to study or engage in technology domestically and that increased number would not meet the demand for the technical knowledge worker. Nor can the government accelerate training for individuals from other professions. The knowledge worker has been in an educational system for many years, excelling at math and problem solving while taking advanced courses. It takes years and certain abilities to excel as a technical knowledge worker. We are at a unique point in time where knowledge work is highly valued (demand) and there are not enough individuals to fill the supply. What happens when demand grossly exceeds supply? Wages and rates will increase, regardless of the economic cycle. If the political tenor continues toward closed borders and protectionism, those individuals and companies with skills domestically will do very well in the coming decade. While demand will increase, companies will still need to find qualified workers and many unqualified consultants and developers will enter the system. Companies will need trusted advisors to help them separate the wheat from the chaff and deliver quality projects driving enterprise value. As an industry and as individuals, we can get involved in local STEM initiatives. If you are a

woman in IT, see how you can contribute to assisting young girls with understanding the benefits of working in a knowledge field. Use your network & influence to drive positive change! One's social capital will be the cornerstone to one's success. Imagine how easy it is for someone to know you have knowledge today, versus the pre-Internet days! It's important to recognize that knowledge alone isn't enough, but that connecting and giving are key to spreading that knowledge around.

In his book *Give and Take,* Adam Grant presents an example of a giver who is at the apex of connecting, and who's social capital is larger than anyone else's). His name is Adam Rifkin, a soft-spoken software developer in Silicon Valley who has started several companies and has a networking group called 106 Miles. This networking group of diverse technology leaders meets monthly in Silicon Valley, San Francisco, and Southern California. In chapter 2 of his book, Grant states, "in 2011 Adam Rifkin had more LinkedIn connections to the 640 most powerful people on *Fortune* magazine's list than any other human being on the planet." Wow! Talk about social capital. How did he do it? Adam still believes his life's work is to be a giver and have a goal of doing acts of kindness for people every day. He wants to change the world by helping others network and connect. In doing so, he has been a tremendous success, helped multiple individuals start companies, and invests an inordinate amount of time helping and networking. His

success speaks for itself. Hypothetically speaking, what if someone wanted to value Rifkin's network; what would it be worth? A million dollars? Ten million? A hundred million? Who knows, but it is easy to say that Rifkin has created an amazing amount of social capital for himself, and for the organizations to which he contributes. That value is not solely in dollars and cents, but also in heartfelt thanks from thousands of individuals who have been positively affected by his acts of kindness. If this humble and introverted software developer from Silicon Valley can be that person, why not you?

Social Media

A good friend of mine, Dipesh Patel, founder of Solvegy a leading-edge strategy and consulting firm, is always tinkering with the latest social media tools. When I met Dipesh, he was a bright analyst and project manager. Because he was involved with a sell and deliver model, I worked with him, notably in his early years. A common perception is that consulting is a glamorous career, and it can be extremely rewarding both financially and intellectually when one is able to solve complex problems. Often, though, the day-to-day equates to three to five people crammed into a small space in a back office of a company. One learns to thwart the world when working and adapts to operating in a small space. One also gets to know colleagues scrupulously. Dipesh was a student of the Networking for Life class I developed. Because he was a classic

introvert, the concepts stretched him. Still he had a thirst for knowledge, asked lots of questions, and faithfully followed the program. This book is for guys like Dipesh. Now, years later, no one would consider Dipesh to be anything but an outgoing and friendly guy, but at heart he is an introvert. He taught himself to be a networker because his entrepreneurial dream was greater than his fear. Dipesh started his own company in 2015 and is still an extraordinary networker.

Somewhere along the line, I became a mentor to Dipesh and others. Most people think mentors pick mentees, but it works just the opposite. A good mentee picks someone who will encourage them, push them, admonish them, and generally be available at any time for a quick question or comment. Often, you don't know you are a mentor. It wasn't until Dipesh started Solvegy, that I realized I was one of his mentors. I did not figure it out until he told me and thanked me. I was equally honored and humbled by his trust. However, today, the roles are reversed because he is guiding me on social media tools and even though I feel like I am with the social media program, one conversation with Dipesh makes me realize that I will need to continue to learn. Dipesh acknowledges that a person never knows what leads will show up in social media. At the time of this writing, he considers today's table stakes to be Snapchat, Twitter, LinkedIn, Instagram, and Facebook. When asked what he means by table stakes he says, "These are the

things you just need to do if you want to be connected online." There are many definitions of table stakes. The term originated in gambling where a person can only win or lose what they placed on the table at the beginning of a hand. In business jargon it means the minimum resources needed to enter a market. According to this definition, we need to be a faithful participant while not really knowing from where the value will come. Just like following the *Connect for Life* principles, sometimes you just have to show up. One must be available – giving, sharing, and helping to find that the harder they work, the luckier they will become.

Dipesh described one lead that appeared in social media right after he updated an item on Facebook about a technology he was exploring. It was not a coincidence that he received an email immediately afterward.

The giving process is not without effort and sacrifice, but everyone who engages in it agrees that the dividend is ten-fold what they invest over time.

On a side note

Proceed with caution on social media as a very accurate picture of you can be developed by those who might want to take advantage or do harm. If you relate this to the process of getting credit, there is an enormous amount of material on the web that describes who an individual is, where they borrow money, where they have lived, etc. One

needs to be careful on the use of passwords, keywords and family names. We all know this but often do not practice safe access. On a recent trip, a friend of my son was recounting a story relayed from his father concerning jury duty. His father had rescheduled his jury duty, yet he received a call the day after the summons specified from an individual who informed him that he had failed to appear for his civic obligation and needed to pay the fine in cash. The call came from an online scammer who spouted scads of information, which made the dad nervous and suspicious. He proceeded to call the court to investigate and report the issue. Bottom line: Always be cautious. Follow some basic rules and know where to draw the line between personal and business information.

Many choose to operate inside of concentric circles. Think about the circles of your life. Personal and business are two different perspectives, but by overlapping those circles, one can leverage time. By engaging in an authentic way with your client, one creates an intimacy that is not easily broken by the newcomer. True relationships create strong connections. When this occurs, social capital is created.

Social media is a necessary element in today's world. Always consider that the principals taught in kindergarten should remain as boundaries toward behaviors. Be nice. Be careful talking to strangers. Speak respectfully even when you disagree with another's position. Say thank you. If you don't have anything good to say, don't say anything at

all. Perhaps you are wondering about the age-old advice, don't talk to strangers. Strangers are strangers if you have never met them in person or have never been introduced. If I get a blind request on LinkedIn, I rarely accept the invite. I view this tool as a vital network where I am lending my contacts to others in order to create social capital. To ensure a reputation stays intact, I don't want to grant access blindly to someone I don't know and allow them a connection in my network.

The other lesson I gleaned from Dipesh is to be on the lookout for new stuff. New technology and ideas are evolving so quickly that one must be proficient at the old stuff in order to recognize the new stuff. Dipesh introduced me to CrystalKnows.com and HubSpot. Crystal uses the DISC personality profile tool to outline how individuals might interact with others. Dipesh accessed this source to generate a report as if he we were going to have an initial encounter. The outline of how we might complement each other, where we might have difficulties, and what strategies could be used to improve a potential first meeting. It was remarkable. Having this insight about an executive prior to the meeting would aid a connector in being more effective in the small amount of time available with a captive audience. It described what the two parties would need to do to *most* effectively communicate. Hubspot, on the other hand, is a quasi-free pipeline management tool that tracks events such as when emails are opened and other types of encounters. There are

various concerns with the volumes of emails assaulting an inbox. I know if I overlook opening email even one day, it is easy to have an important email that I have received disappear amongst the clutter of other emails. Simply knowing if an email has been opened or not is an advantage that can help you devise your follow-up plan. Portions of Hubspot's platform are licensed, and other modules are free. There are many more of these software platforms, which could provide leverage in the social media camp.

The point is that social media is often the initial place today where connections happen. But if you stop there, you have missed the boat. Never forget that social media tools are there to enable us to have a human or personal encounter. At some point, one has to connect face to face and exchange value. That's how it works. We are now able to source technical resources from every corner of the planet and there are many smaller consulting firms popping up all over the country who specialize in something like strategy (Thought Ensemble), strategy and technology (Solvegy), offshore support and near shore consulting (Cyber Group), user experience (Saltbox), business and technology (Trans4mative), outsourced CIO (Comport), project management and technology (W3management), and the list goes on. What is changing in the industry is that trusted networks of solution providers are increasingly being utilized by companies. In the last four years, I have sourced almost

every company on the above list to my current inventory of projects. Even if a monetary contract was not implemented, I certainly called the company founders for insight and advice on specific topics. I am evidence that I am a better advisor because of my network and my clients benefit from those connections. The value increases exponentially. The fact that talented individuals are leaving larger companies to start smaller enterprises is largely facilitated by both social media and connecting. Because demand is high for these services, individuals choose to specialize in something where they excel, and they discover profitability at the same time. When they connect to others, it creates a loosely defined network of solution providers. It becomes a community that is built on trust. If you are the hub of that network enormous value can be brought to your client. I believe this is the wave of the future. Connecting is more important than ever and will become the value creator for businesses in the years to come as technology accelerates, complexity increases, and businesses need help to sort it all out.

Chapter 5 - Beyond Connecting

About 20 years ago a friend of mine met with a prospective client who was interested in the service my friend's company offered. My friend's company was a technology consulting firm that specialized in Microsoft technologies and he was vice president of sales. The prospect was a publisher looking to implement various strategies to lower cost and improve efficiencies. My friend had done the research and was able to schedule a meeting with the prospect. Just as the meeting got underway, and before the small talk began, the prospect painted a very competitive environment for selling and delivering services to his company. They were cutthroat and only cared about price. As the meeting progressed, the prospect's phone rang, and in less than five minutes the meeting was over.

Afterward my friend followed up, left messages, and . . . nothing. He remembered that he had a good rapport with the prospect and thought it odd that there was no reception to his desire to follow-up. Then my friend remembered the prospect mentioning that he and his wife enjoyed eggs Benedict. My friend found a restaurant near his prospect's office that served eggs Benedict. He went to investigate the establishment to ensure their food was tasty and consistent. He then dangled the breakfast carrot to the prospect and asked if he could shake

away and meet him one morning for breakfast. The prospect agreed to the meeting and they finally got together. By the end of the meal, the prospect asked if any of the business items he discussed (at their previous meeting) were in the core competency of my friend's company, which happened to be the principal concern. A truthful reply of yes led to a lifelong friendship and business relationship.

This is one of many stories relayed to me about a relationship turning into a business value exchange. Since then this client has found value in the solutions my friend's company provided, and the client has emphasized to my friend that having a relationship built on trust is the most important thing to him. Once that trust was established, it spilled over into both the business and personal realm. The happily ever after is, they ate eggs Benedict once a month at that same restaurant for eight years after that initial meeting.

Establishing a trusted relationship and then edging into a sales opportunity requires some time and well-developed skills. First, you must genuinely be a giver and must want to help someone else without expecting anything in return. You must be a person with emotional intelligence who tries to empathize with the needs of your customers and prospects. Emotional intelligence allows you to sense intuitively what is going on around you. For some people this is easy. Others need to translate actions and feelings into information that can be processed into

behaviors and actions. Those actions and understanding of others are the cornerstone of trust. In virtually every good relationship, one quality that exists between individuals is empathy. To form a relevant bond with others, you must be empathetic to what is going on in their world.

One of the most used and least understood phrases is *pain points*. In his book, *Solution Selling, Creating Buyers in Difficult Selling Markets*, Michael Bosworth describes how a seller needs to foster latent pain to pain (defined below) before he or she can cultivate a vision for a solution. In this process, the seller asks open-ended questions to find out what problem is festering under the surface. I constantly ask my teams, "What is the problem we are trying to solve?" Bosworth claims there are three steps:

1. Uncovering the problem (latent pain).
2. Making it real. (It has to become real pain that has a value associated with making it go away.)
3. Giving the buyer a vision of a solution that might eliminate the problem from the business.

I have worked with hundreds of people who can uncover a pain point. But most people when they uncover the pain do not show empathy to the problem nor determine the depth of the problem in the eyes of the buyer. They quickly rush into the solution they perceive the buyer needs, which happens to be the solution they are being paid to sell.

In short, unless you are empathetic and authentic it is difficult to know a pain point even when it hits you between the eyes. It has been my experience that most people feel sales people are predatory. If the process is not done correctly, with empathy and authenticity, it will come off as self-serving and will create mistrust, the opposite of trust. You will also lose the opportunity. To be truly successful, you need to think about how to be world-class at developing relationships. If you are empathetic and care about the outcome for your client, the sales will be greater, and you will solve many more complex problems. With that, your reputation will grow and thus, your personal success.

Once you have built that relationship, shown you care, and earned the client's trust, the relationship is firmly established for life. Trust is a delicate thing that cannot be violated, ever. Once you have trust, you become a steward of that trust, and as you explore your network for the kind of problems you are uniquely qualified to solve, then the magic begins to happen.

How to Earn and Keep Credibility

As with any relationship, you must continue to be credible. You earn credibility when you say and do honest, credible things.

For example:

- Being both punctual and professional
- Being honest about what your company can and cannot do

- Recommending someone else in your network, when you are not a fit
- Accurately describing your team's strengths and weaknesses
- Confronting problems and being honest, especially when you make a mistake
- Asking difficult questions and telling them why you need the answer
- Thanking them for their help

Building the Connection

Part of building relationships involves maintaining regular contact.

Regular contact is what turns networking into connecting. I'll say that

again. *REGULAR CONTACT IS WHAT TURNS NETWORKING INTO*

CONNECTING. If you neglect a client who has trust in your integrity as a

person, that client may feel like you only care about them for the

business aspect of your relationship. You need to make yourself

available through several methods of contact, and have a system in

place that you use regularly. Are you joined on LinkedIn? I am sure you

are. So are 433 million other people. That is not being connected. Do

you have their cell number and have you texted them lately? I would

guess that an average IT executive receives over 100 emails a day. I

would also guess that they receive fewer than 10 text messages. Which

is more intimate?

Let's talk for a moment about how to do these things with

authenticity and not create a feeling of manipulation. You will find this

has an abundance to do with giving. Good leaders are givers. They

serve. Think about your current mindset regarding building long-term relationships, both internally and externally to the firm. Discuss with your peers how your thinking has evolved over time. In his book *Love is the Killer App*, Tim Sanders introduces the concept of being a *love cat*. What is a love cat? It is someone who shares their knowledge freely, shares their network and shares their compassion. To be a love cat, you must take a genuine interest in others. It cannot be faked. I have had periods in my career where I was excellent at networking with companies and partners in the local market. Then, I went to work in the precious metals business and the entire notion of my network changed. My technology contacts were still very relevant, as we needed to build new platforms for precious metals trading. The difference was the customer base. Because the company is a global precious metals wholesaler, the reach of their clients is far and wide. There would never have been a reason in the past for me to come across any of their customers. I had to start from scratch. It occurred to me one day that I was going to have to get on the road and go from dealer to dealer until I knew a critical mass of clients. There was no short cut to learning the business from the customer's perspective. I was going to have to be a love cat in a strange land. By asking a lot of questions, I would be able to understand their many challenges and establish rapport. We had created an entirely new trading platform for our customers that would make their lives better for the

buying and selling of precious metals. They were not on LinkedIn, and they did not particularly like technology . . . so I hit the road. One by one I met them by walking through the front door, putting out my hand and making a friend. I would plan a trip every other month, and for about a year and a half I flew, drove, and called my way around the world until I had established relationships. Along the way, we got great feedback, which drove the requirements for the platform and a keen appreciation for showing up and thanking them for their business. I think Tim Sanders would call that love cat behavior.

While my new network began to thrive, my old network began to atrophy. I realized that I needed to engage in reestablishing my old network without anyone feeling like there was an ulterior motive. I took time every day to send a message on LinkedIn or a text to tell my contacts that I was thinking about them and was sorry that I'd fallen into a hole. I asked if they had time for a quick phone call to catch up. When we did get together on the phone or in person over a meal, it was me asking them how they were, what their family was up to, and if there was anything I could do to help. Another former colleague, who had started a new company in Houston, asked if I would be available to coach and mentor him as he navigated his start-up technology business. Another person became a vendor to my current company, which led to an invitation for me to serve on their board. You have to be involved in the

game for good things to happen, and you have to do it with an authentic heart and the intention of being a giver.

Chapter 6 - Touch Points

Going to the next level requires effort in order to be successful, but most importantly, you need a plan and a method of tracking your progress against that plan. Creating touch points is an effort to chronicle the most important activities necessary to build a network and then begin to transition this network into a source of sales leads and prospective business for your company. This is usually one of the most difficult activities to keep up consistently throughout the year. If you remember Stephen Covey's admonishment from *The Seven Habits of Highly Effective People*, we should all focus on the *important* over the *urgent* in our daily lives, but this is difficult. We tend to get busy working deals (urgent) and stop doing the basics of pipeline management (important).

Pipeline management is the lifeblood of any company. A sales pipeline is a list of qualified opportunities that if closed will generate revenue for your company. Managing a pipeline through a step-by-step process is critical to success. With every opportunity being tracked, one should list the company's name, the key contact, the type of solution being offered from your portfolio, the size of the opportunity, and the probability of winning. At each stage, there is information to consider to

help gauge the level of progress in the sale. If potential revenue-producing opportunities are exhausted, you are dead. It doesn't matter whether you are a for-profit or a non-profit organization since a steady flow of opportunities is required for revenue generation. A pipeline provides prospects, but most importantly a pipeline provides preferable posture in dealing with existing prospects. In every opportunity there comes a time when the question must be asked, "Should I walk away from this deal?" Walking away gets easier if there is something else to walk toward. I challenge the people I'm coaching with a simple phrase – "three is not twenty." If you only have three prospects, you will annoy them, and they will begin to sense your desperation. When you realize that you have something special to offer and the client will be better off if they use your offering, your posture and confidence will increase. As your posture increases along with the size of your pipeline, you will focus on the best opportunities that represent the greatest fit. You win, the client wins, and the job becomes incredibly rewarding.

Developing touch points will help you be successful by identifying the base level activity that leads to prosperous connections. You need to determine what activities are consequential to track. They can be named, assigned a value, and tracked week to week. Peter Drucker was famous for saying "what gets measured gets managed." His advice still rings true.

Part of the *Connect for Life* methodology exists in our software platform called Touchpoints. The software enables individuals to develop their own unique activities, then manage and track the activities as the user improves as a connector. Eventually, it will be evident which activities have the most value and lead to success. At the enterprise level, this can be presented to every employee and aggregate activity accordingly.

This might be more suitable than a pipeline report.

Classification	Activity	Description	Points
Networking	Message	Reach out to a contact via email or social media	1
Networking	Appointment	Meet in person or on a scheduled phone call	2
Networking	Event	Attend a networking event	3
Networking	Publish	Write a blog or submit an article to be published	3
Networking	Speak	Speak at an event on your expertise	5
Connecting	Linkage	Send an idea to a friend, colleague, or prospect	1
Connecting	Introduction	Introduce someone in your network to someone else in your network	2
Connecting	Advise	Do something for someone in your network by providing expertise for free	3
Connecting	Give	Do something for someone that would represent "paying it forward"	3
Selling	Call	Contact someone in a key account to get a first meeting	1
Selling	Pitch	Create something to leave behind at an account	2
Selling	Meeting	Have a meeting at an account or with an individual	2
Selling	Proposal	Create a proposal for the account	2
Selling	Meeting C	Any C-suite meeting	3
Selling	Close	Be part of a closing meeting where the deal is agreed upon	5

The graphic above illustrates 15 activities that reinforce networking and sales success. This is just an initial list with a point value assigned to each activity. At first, it might not be a priority to track all of these activities, in fact, start with basic touches to establish a habit. However, if the aspiration is to progress from being a networker to a

connector to a seller, a clear understanding of these three processes is necessary.

Processes Defined - The idea here is to create a master list of touch points that will serve as a starting position as you begin your journey. The software that complements this book will allow for modification of categories to suit your industry and sales process. You will also be able to tweak the points assigned to each activity. The idea is to keep it simple, yet broad enough to lead to success. The following section explains more about the activities in the previous graphic.

Networking – the act of spreading one's personal brand and investing in a marketplace. Think of networking like an action word. This is not a short-term process. It is a life-long process. They say it takes 10,000 hours to become a master, but it will take far less to be a proficient networker. Networking is the foundation for one's personal brand.

> **Message** – There will be many opportunities to send messages to individuals in your network. Set aside time every morning, evening, or weekend to keep your contacts fresh. Even your coldest contacts in your network should be messaged every six to twelve months.

> **Appointment** –Meeting at a scheduled time is important in networking. This can be on the phone or in person. I use the phrase, "would you like to grab a cup of coffee," when I am

asking a busy person for 10 minutes of their time. This tends to sound less daunting to both parties. A cup of coffee can be short or long, depending on the quality of the conversation. If the conversation is interesting, a busy executive will always find more time. Try this strategy prior to more costly lunches and dinners.

Events – Choose events wisely. Make sure that you pick events where meaningful one-on-one dialogue with key people can occur. Otherwise, one can get evented to death as there is always something going on. You will be busy and fall into the trap of confusing activity with accomplishment. Have a goal for each event you attend. Whether it is to learn a new concept that you can share with clients or meeting a specific person to whom you have wanted to be introduced. Have a plan.

Publish – These days it is easy to publish something such as an article, a blog, or a podcast. Write about something relative to your expertise and become an expert. This is more of a pull strategy as people in your network will pull you into conversations that will lead to opportunities. As a knowledge worker, spend time each week thinking of giving your ideas away. Most companies need help implementing any new ideas they read about.

Speak – The fastest way to create a personal brand is to speak at an event relative to your expertise. If you are deeply technical, this is an easy way to begin to develop your social capital. If the subject is around your domain knowledge, it will be easier for you to communicate.

Connecting – the act of selflessly giving to one's network and connections. It is helping without the desire for reciprocity. It is believing that if you give away what you have, it will be revisited on you tenfold. Your relationships and connections will help you because you have first given selflessly to them.

Linkage – As you read newspapers, peruse the web, read books, and have conversations with others, pass this knowledge on to connections in your network. One of the most valuable gifts you can give to someone in your network is an edge because of the knowledge that you provided. Linkage means you were thinking about them when you read something and thought to pass it on. It doesn't always have to be a major thing. I once called a friend who worked in Paris for five years and asked him for advice for a family trip I was planning. He gave us two or three activities and a few off-the-beaten-path places to visit. Our family still talks about that advice.

Introduction – Most of what you should be doing in your network is helping others to succeed. Often, this will be a simple introduction to someone in your network. Tim Sanders says always share your network with anyone who asks.

Advise – Give away what you know, especially if you are in the business of selling that knowledge for a profit. It could be something simple to you, but it will mean a lot to your connection. Track this consistently.

Give – By paying it forward, you will help others with their needs. Do not worry about your needs. Becoming an active giver will pay you back far more than you can ever give away. Just the concept alone of paying it forward requires a giver's attitude and faith in the future.

Selling – the act of matching a company's need to a solution that one can deliver. Not just presenting a solution but taking a prospect through a sales process where it becomes clear that they should choose you. If you actively network and connect you will have a pipeline of prospects; however, the art of selling requires an understanding of techniques necessary during a sales process. This will be addressed in more detail in the second half of the book.

Call – You will never get to the next step in the selling process if you do not call. You can save much time if you plot out how to

make the call and to make it to the right person. When you are trying to get into an account, it is prudent to start with someone in your network (warm contact) who might give you an introduction to a person or company. People will help you with an email introduction or they may pick up the phone and call the person you want to meet. Take their lead in describing the best approach and then always follow-up with them to tell them what happened. It is a common courtesy to follow up with a quick note or a handwritten thank you.

Pitch – Having a conversation and fostering dialogue with a prospect is generally more effective than a presentation. With so many sellers it is like a gun goes off and their mouth starts running. One will learn more when their mouth is closed, and the prospect's is open. It is effective to have something to leave behind or an item (like a printed slideshow) to which you can refer to make a point. Remember the pitch deck stays around and sells even after you have left the appointment, but don't lead with it.

Meeting – Every sales process begins with a meeting. Always take a meeting in person if you can, as this is where trust and rapport are established. Always gratefully accept a cup of coffee or water and walk with them to the kitchen. Much can be inferred

by observing the culture surrounding a prospect. Keep in mind that a buyer has an advantage today because of the information available through the web and social media. One needs to come up to speed in learning as fast as possible. Always schedule the next meeting before the current one is over. The purpose of a meeting is to get another meeting!

Follow-up – There are follow-ups at the account level and at the individual level. Follow-up is where most people lose the deal. Microsoft did a study of its sales force and found that it took, on average, twelve touches for a company to win. Most sales people give up on the 3rd or 4th try. Perseverance is rewarded for a reason.

Meeting "C" – Getting access to power is critical to the success of any pursuit, whether a new prospect or an existing client. The C-suite is a term used to describe senior executives empowered to make decisions, usually corporate officers whose titles begin with "chief." Tracking how often one makes contact with an executive is important. You will become proficient in negotiating your way into the C-suite.

Proposal – The proposal is a very strategic step in an account. It is the beginning of the true sales process and will be covered in great length later in this book. The methodology says to always

lead with a pre-proposal before the final proposal. The pre-proposal, usually a slide show presentation rather than a document, allows a discussion around the ideas you have, your understanding of the problem and a range of fees and timeline. This way, the prospect can modify what you have provided before you send a final proposal.

Close – Closing a deal is where the revenue comes from and the persuasion is confirmed. Not all closings are for products or services. Sometimes you are closing the next step in the sales cycle. For example, if getting the right people at the right meeting is part of your strategy, then accomplishing that step is very important.

Additional Activities - A few other things that you might want to consider giving some points on are the following:

Continuing Education – Attending some form of continuing education class that pertains to your industry or your market focus can prove valuable. This may be a class at your local university or community college that will give you an edge above others. You can stream podcasts and audible books to your phone and turn your drive time into a university level program. A recent article in Fortune magazine says that the average

commute time in the top 50 cities is approximately 30 minutes. Imagine adding 8 to 10 hours of learning to your weekly goals!

Trade Shows – Depending on your industry and how often these shows occur, you can view this as a networking event, and you can create a goal for touch points at the event.

Review Points - If you are working on a little friendly competition with colleagues, conduct weekly meetings with all the participants (over lunch or via conference call) to discuss progress and ideas about how to improve your performance and improve the contest. If you remember my experience with the Big Dawg contest, that little bit of friendly competition and accountability was critical to establishing a habit. If you are trying to drive pipeline activity for a larger group, a weekly meeting that reviews aggregate touch points and pipeline activities will prove to be effective.

Rewards - Whether you are doing this as an individual or as a group, reward yourself as you start this process. Rewards can be as insignificant as a cold drink, to a day off, or something more important based upon a goal. You should have a system of rewards in the moment, so if you make five phone calls you reward yourself. If you hit 100 points (as outlined in the chart on page 75) in a month, reward yourself with something bigger.

The Heat Map

With Touchpoints, you can see a heat map around your activities or the activities of a larger group. In this illustration, a user can see the goals that were set in the past. This way the user can determine if the goals are being reached across the three dimensions – networking, connecting, and selling.

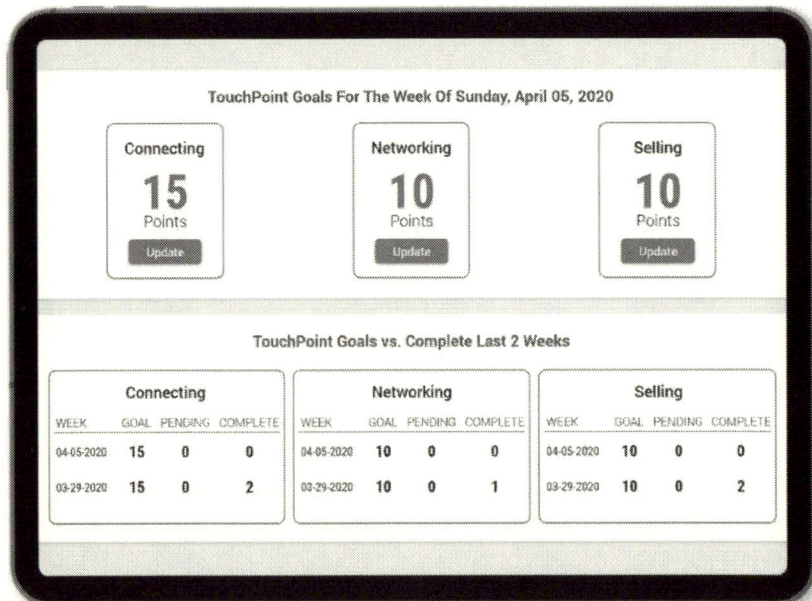

By understanding what works and what does not, you can tweak and change the model to optimize it for yourself or for your organization. For example, if you compare the following two graphs, you might find that for a period of six months, the graphic on the left represents your touch point count. Then for 90 days you really get serious about connecting and the resulting activity goes up substantially.

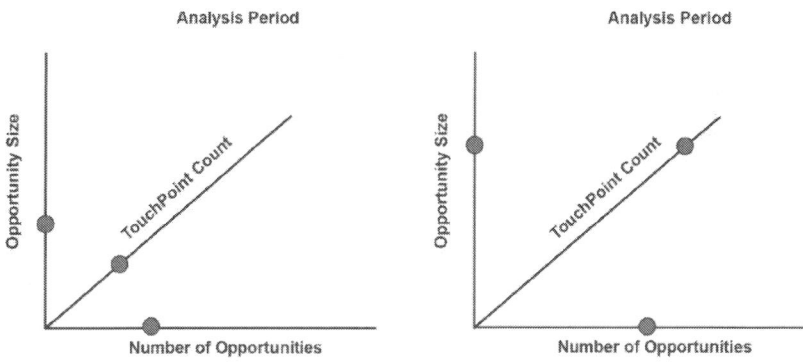

The results would show you how both your opportunity size and the number of opportunities you are pursuing continues to increase. Touchpoints software focuses on delivering analytics that provide feedback at a detailed level, so progress can be addressed. Conceivably, you could have more breakfast meetings or more warm introductions from your network. Over time, it would be reasonable to improve both the quality and quantity of your meetings.

Consider account management within an existing client. Maybe a goal was to take someone at the company to drinks or lunch and to

become better acquainted. Perhaps you find out that you have an activity in common like riding bikes or roller blading. Or maybe you both like music. Once you find those common interests, you can further the relationship. Start blogging on a new technology, and you may gain a gathering of individuals inside of the company connecting with you on the blog. Publish a document or co-write it with someone in the client's organization. These are just a few ways to develop overlapping circles of business and social interaction with people you enjoy being with. For most consultants, managing one's connections at an existing account is time well spent. Without a doubt, a system should be established to reinforce good habits. Today, it is hard to find tools which help the connector manage high value activities. In each unique situation, the high value activities must be determined. Then committing to monitoring that activity on a regular basis will lead to personal growth and success.

Within many organizations, there is the notion of hunters and farmers. The hunter is an individual who is adept at selling new clients, where the farmer is the person who is adept at edging into new divisions at a company. Regardless of the way the effort is characterized, the activity is the same. It's just that one activity is outside the four walls of a single company (hunter), and the other is inside (farmer). Both activities are equally important and critical to the health and survival of a business.

To create value, you have to connect. If this progression is not monitored, it is difficult to continuously sharpen the saw.

There goes a story of a lumberjack in East Texas who was very skilled at the process of felling trees. He was a legend and had a record of 18 trees in one working day. As he aged, there was a line of young lumberjacks who would show up and try to beat his record. One day, a strapping young man showed up at the camp and went to work trying to prove his mettle. He woke early and went into the woods and by the time he came back to camp, he had felled 14 trees. The camp rallied with the news. The old record holder pulled up a chair next to our young buck and said, "Nice work son, you got close." With a glean in his eye, the young lumberjack looked at his elder and said, "Tomorrow, I'll start earlier and go later."

Once again, into the evening the young buck chopped trees and down they came. Well into the evening he walked into the camp with his head held low and dejected. One lumberjack yelled to him, "How many?" To which the young man replied, "twelve." What a disappointment. He went backwards. Nevertheless, he ate a good dinner and vowed to get up earlier and work later the next day.

The next evening, even later than the previous, the young man walked into camp having felled 10 trees. He sat dejected at the dinner table fumbling with his food. At just the right moment the elder

lumberjack sauntered over to where the young man was sitting. Their eyes met, and the younger man looked at the old guy and said, "I just don't get it." The elder lumberjack paused for a moment and said, "Son, at any time in the last three days, have you stopped to sharpen your axe?" The young man understood and shook his head.

How many of us fail to sharpen our axe in business or in our personal lives? The sharpening stone for our axes is tracking the touch points one has on a daily, weekly, and monthly basis. As stated in previous chapters, you cannot manage what you do not measure. The same is true of connecting. You must define what you want to track and why it is a priority. Then it must be measured against a goal or a target. This paradigm is simple and difficult at the same time.

Chapter 7 - Made or Born

If this is your first exposure to the concept of networking or sales, a personal bias or aversion may have to be conquered. My palms were sweaty when I started in sales. I started with a model in my head that closely resembled the experience I had when I purchased my first car at an auto dealership. I hated it, and the process became indelible in my mind. Many of you have had the same experience. Your brain has locked that feeling into a long-term, things-to-avoid, list. So here is the challenge. One can remain in fear, or else rise up and seize the day.

When I hear it said that someone is a natural born salesperson, I laugh at the cliché. There are intricate details, processes, and connections that are necessary to win in today's highly competitive world. Learning these details is not rocket science, and it is not as hard as mastering your chosen profession. Most of the, "naturally born sales people," apply themselves to their craft and practice, practice, practice. Recall Vince Lombardi's statement, "Practice does not make perfect, only perfect practice makes perfect." In a word, they are professionals. If you want results, you have to commit to doing the work.

In *Solution Selling*, Bosworth describes the application of the 80/20 rule to selling, where 20% of sales people produce 80% of the results. He calls these people eagles, while I have referred to them as natural born sellers. Bosworth mentions that these individuals are largely

unable to transfer their skills to others. The premise of his book, which I agree with 100%, is that "a good Journeyman can be trained to consistently outsell an Eagle salesman who is winging it." Wikipedia defines a Journeyman as follows, "A journeyman is a skilled worker who has successfully completed an official apprenticeship qualification in a building trade or craft. Journeymen are considered competent and authorized to work in that field as a fully qualified employee." In his quest to solve this problem, he wrote the book *Solution Selling,* which became widely adopted in the enterprise software selling industry during the Y2K crisis of 1999. Companies raced to convert their accounting and other systems because many of them were not capable of handling the date 2000. Previously, developers had always programmed the date field as 19XX, by hard coding the 19. When a system clock ticked over from 1999 at 11:59pm, the system would be unable to process year 2000 and the system would crash. This is why people defined the problem as Year 2K (K=1,000), and Y2K was created. The competition was fierce in selling these applications, and software companies sought to scale their sales forces by teaching *Solution Selling* workshops. It was very effective.

When I talk to consultants (mostly introverted and technical), the concept of sales is foreign, but process is comforting. I tell them to remember, it is a process, and they are good at processes. They have

been following processes all their technical lives. In fact, they probably have an opinion about good processes versus bad processes. It doesn't matter if a person is an engineer, an architect, a software developer, or an attorney, processes are your friend. Also, by establishing a common process across a company of knowledge workers, the organization establishes a common language for describing how to prosecute a deal.

I remember the point in my sales career when I finally realized that there was a pattern for success. Patterns in technology and software development are very commonplace in the lingo of engineers. Because I was not taught any basic sales paradigm or technique, I looked at a sales cycle as if it was a project I had to manage. Along with the revelation that I needed to sell to the right kind of prospects; I also started seeing the patterns that worked within a sales cycle.

I have heard phrases like, "necessity is the mother of invention" and "frustration is the father of progress." Both are true, but repetition is the mother skill. If you follow this program and repeat it over time, you will succeed. Regardless of what the world tells you, sales people are made, not born. Yes, there are the occasional few who are in the right place at the right time and seem to succeed so easily, and yet if asked to articulate how it happened, they generally cannot tell you. They have the feel but can't describe a process. Every individual has more to offer than they ever imagined. The principle must be driven home that when the

customer wins, the seller automatically wins as well. One must commit to the program. If you commit to the program, the rewards will automatically follow.

Winning also rewards significantly better than losing. When one is on commission, you are a funded entrepreneur by the company. They pay for your space, equipment, and travel with zero financial risk to you. There is no prize for second place. I was not born an eagle salesperson in Bosworth's nomenclature, but I banged my head against the wall until I figured it out. Then, over the last 15 years, I started to record this process, so others like you can make your own march from Journeyman to eagle.

Chapter 8 - Forgiveness

To be a success, one must have both talent and persistence, and the ability to forgive oneself when mistakes are made. Let's talk about talent. We've all heard the phrase, "It doesn't matter what you know, it's who you know." This statement is both true and false. If you are selling a complex solution, you must have knowledge particular to that complex solution. If an engineer builds a bridge that collapses, or if a software developer cannot compile a program, they may have picked the wrong profession. Failure would be in the future of those individuals.

As a professional, one needs to believe in continuous improvement. A knowledge worker knows that the work is hard, but they know that there are rewards associated with the hard work; thus, they endeavor to get better. Some of the careers outlined in this book (technology, engineering, law, etc.) require advanced schooling. People who have successfully finished the rigor of a university bachelor's or master's program, also have persistence because they pushed through the many challenges that come with a higher education.

I wrestled in high school, and I knew that when you saw the ceiling tiles, there was less than a second to get moving in a different direction. If there was a pause, or a hesitation, inevitably you would hear the whistle and a slap of the referee's hand. That slap meant for that

moment, you quit. Vince Lombardi once said, "Quitters never win and winners never quit," and it is true. Even when knocked down, winners continue to get up. Failure is a great teacher. Rarely do we learn from success, which is why I tell people to fail fast and get back in the game.

I remember a failure that had a profound impact on my life. Millburn High School in Millburn, New Jersey, had an outstanding reputation as a wrestling school with a winning tradition. The school had many outstanding wrestlers who contended at the state level – Bill Miron, Buzz Wagonseller, Mike Kaufman, Mark Serruto, and Paul Finn, to name a few. I grew up down the street from Roger Serruto, Mark's younger brother. Roger and I were best friends as youngsters, and my interest in wrestling grew from being around Roger's five brothers. In seventh and eighth grade, two of his older brothers were our coaches in the township league. All my best friends were on that team and many are still friends today.

In my junior year I played football, wrestled, and ran track. I had a bad shoulder that gave me issues from time to time, and my buddies affectionately called me "lemon face" when I would grimace in pain. I had made first team all-conference my junior football season, and I was in contention to be all-conference in the 400-yard dash for track. As I recall, we had a good wrestling team our junior year. I don't recall losing a conference match all year. Our coach Jerry Sachsel was a legend at

Millburn High School. He served as the first wrestling coach from 1965 to 1980 and accumulated a record of 161 (wins), 36 (losses) and 3 (ties). He coached three of Millburn's State Champions: Bill Miron, Buzz Wagonseller, and Paul Finn. Mr. Sachsel was a demanding coach with a quiet demeanor, but when he spoke one listened. Mr. Sachsell was a champion in his own right winning two state championships for his high school. His dual meet record in high school and college was 60-0 and 2. That means in team competition, he never lost in eight years of high school and college. A very impressive record.

Our locker room had an anonymous quote on the wall that stated, "Remember, when you are not working, there is someone else who is, and when you meet him, he will beat you." It was a program steeped in tradition. Wrestling is equivalent in New Jersey to what Texans call Friday night lights. The entire town shuts down and everyone shows up to cheer on the home team. Just remembering those times brings chills.

I was undefeated in the conference, and we were going up against West Orange. I don't remember my opponent's name, but he was built and looked stronger than me, and that got inside my head. Early in the match, I shot (the activity of trying to take your opponent down to the mat) and he sprawled back (the activity of trying not to be taken down to the mat) just as my right shoulder was extended. I had

previously separated my shoulder, and I felt it pop, but not separate. It hurt but I continued wrestling. While I was probably the better technical wrestler, I lost that match 6 – 4. Our team won the meet and after showering, Coach Sachsel asked to talk to me once everyone had gone home. He was a man of few words. I don't remember exactly what he said, but it went something like this, "You were better than he was. Are you hurt or injured?" I said, "Just hurt." He said, "I don't ever want to see a grimace on your face on these mats unless you are injured. I think you gave up!"

Oh man, that went right through the heart. Then, he went on to say, "Did you realize that if you had beaten him today, you had the potential to be all-conference in all three sports as a junior? Did you also know that no one has ever accomplished that in the history of Millburn High School? Never give up, son. You are not a quitter!" With that, he walked down the hallway. I stood there stunned.

Just like perseverance can be learned, so too can quitting. There comes a time in every personal journey when one has to push through or get off the mat. As you work through this material, there might be an insecure thought or even the inclination to want to quit. In addition to the two prerequisites, talent and persistence, you need to be honest with yourself and be capable of self-forgiveness. Remember the 11th

commandment, "Thou shall not kid thyself".. Do not for a second fool yourself.

When one starts tracking Touchpoints, the temptation may exist to focus on getting points instead of doing meaningful activity. Never confuse activity with accomplishment. It happens every day, but you must check the data and ask yourself if you are confusing activity with accomplishment. If the answer is yes, get up and start again. You are the only one who can erase the slate and start over. There will be areas where you will struggle but stick with it. This is why forgiveness is such a critical quality to embrace. When we think of forgiveness we often think of forgiving others. Forgiveness is powerful because it says to the other person that the slate is wiped clean and nothing is owed. When you think about getting off track, not reaching your goals, or being pinned in a wrestling match, forgiveness is necessary to keep you from quitting on your future.

Everyone makes mistakes. Successful entrepreneurs, investors, and sales people fail more than others. I recently listened to a weekly podcast by *Real Vision*, a financial news source. They have a segment called "Things I Got Wrong," where they interview many of the most influential money managers and investors in the world. The people interviewed are the best of the best managing billions of dollars for their clients. Invariably, the interviewer gets to the question that goes

something like, "Do you remember a scenario that you can share where an investment or trade lost money?" All who are interviewed invariably giggle when they hear the question because they have all made big mistakes. In the most recent episode they interviewed Michael Lewitt, a famous author and investor. He said, "If you haven't made a mistake, you are not a true investor." He went on to tell a story about how his company turned a $2 million-dollar loss into a $10 million-dollar loss when they tried to fix a company with a flawed business model. Mr. Lewitt said, "Sometimes your first loss is your cheapest loss." Do you think Mr. Lewitt had to forgive himself before he could get back in the game? You bet. As a CFO friend of mine likes to say, "In football, a cornerback has to have a short memory." This means that if somebody catches a ball for a touchdown or a long gain, the cornerback, whose job it was to stop the play, has to forget about it and prepare for the next play. I tend not to trust anyone who has not been kicked in the teeth a few times. Try to fail fast, forgive yourself, and get back in the game.

Chapter 9 - The End Game

All things being equal, people would rather buy from people they know and trust. If you are a person of high integrity and talent, why wouldn't you want to share solutions with your network? As I previously stated, this is a process. As you master networking and connecting, you will eventually progress to selling. There are more people involved in selling in America than any other profession. Regardless of your profession, everyone must sell every day. Anyone who has children, attended a university, participated on a team, or pushed an important initiative at work has been engaged in sales. For example, when my kids were younger, my wife and I worked on instilling in them the principles of hard work and doing their best. Because children are usually interested in having fun and getting immediate gratification rather than fulfilling their obligations, they would rather watch TV than do homework if left to their own devices. Kids are a tough sell. Make no mistake, as sellers, we are continually reinforcing the principles we valued as family so that our children can grow up and find success in life.

I recall a client who was implementing a new enterprise resource planning system (ERP) where the lack of internal selling by the CIO caused the project to be in jeopardy. As we continued to face delays I sat with the CFO and told him that the project would expand to fill the

time allotted and he needed to pick a go-live date for the new software.

His response was that the system still had bugs and the users were not

trained. I said, "And in a month, we will be facing the same

circumstances." He chose a date and the employees rallied around the

date. In the end, the testing team found critical flaws in the software and

the project was suspended indefinitely. Had we not set a date and

pushed hard, we would never have found out what the real issues were.

Often, these mini sales cycles need the use of moral suasion,

but that is just a fancy phrase for internal selling. We make our point,

present the facts, rally support, and work to implement our point of view.

Whether for the team or the family, make no mistake, these activities all

involve selling.

I remember selling an enterprise software package to a company

that would improve order management, distribution, and accounting for

that firm. This system, when implemented, would allow them to grow

their business without adding headcount. The project was progressing

and the team was working through the weekend to try to get some of the

final modules configured. The project manager called me and said that

she could not get to the client that Saturday because someone had run

over her mailbox and she needed to get it fixed. I told her that I would fix

it and she could go to the client site and manage the project. I fixed the

mailbox; she helped the project go live. There became a great story

around the company about how a sales guy fixed a mailbox so their project could go live.

Four years later, that same company was our first customer at the consulting firm I started in 2003. I called the president and said, "I just quit my job, and I need a client." He hired me. You never know when your effort will pay off. Selling is about helping people and companies achieve their business objectives and doing so with the utmost integrity. This is why I call sales an honorable profession.

Following this plan will lead to the most rewarding outcomes. Every person on the planet has something special to share or has a unique skill that can be leveraged to help people. Go ahead, *Connect for Life* and watch your life change.

PART TWO – The Basics

In the second half of this book, we will transition from our connecting process to developing strategies to use to solve problems inside of an enterprise. Once you commit and apply yourself to connecting and being a giver, the hard part is over. As you continue to work as a connector, people will seek you out because of your expertise and ability to solve problems. Opportunities will arise because you are the only one with a particular expertise and are consistently connecting with your network. When connectors continuously meet with those in their networks, they become top of mind to those people, which leads to being contacted more often. That will translate into greater opportunities giving the connector an advantage in a sales cycles. Understanding these basics taught to sales people will enable the connector to create more effective strategies for winning.

You do not need to go out and read the top 10 books on sales, although it would be a good idea. Knowledge, techniques, and artifacts that are consistent with the information shared in those books have already been gleaned and disbursed throughout the rest of this book. Then, these artifacts are assembled in such a way as to provide understanding and continuity to the sales process. Think of it like

weaving a sales tapestry from the best thinkers and techniques available today and delivering it in a concise manner.

Chapter 10 - Telling Stories

The technician whose career has been spent in the minute details of a solution might conclude that success is about conveying additional information and knowledge. "If I can just give them a little more information, they will see what I mean." Unfortunately, this approach does not always work. Effective connectors are good storytellers. For centuries, stories were the fabric of families, communities, and countries. Before the printing press, there was only storytelling. People groups learned their history by listening to their elders -- what a concept. The best sellers relate stories of how a similar customer had that same problem as the prospect, and how the seller's company helped solve that problem. My dilemma early in my sales management career was how to teach others the art of storytelling. It wasn't until I read a book by Ford Harding called *Creating Rainmakers,* where he introduced the concept of using anecdotes, that I understood there is a process to storytelling. Finally, a formula for telling a story that could be taught and conveyed from teacher to seller to prospect to client. Much of what follows in this chapter was learned from his book.

Successful sellers have used anecdotes for years, but the question is, "Why is it necessary to use anecdotes?" Regardless of what one sells, tangible or intangible, buyers still want proof of success. The

nature of solution selling is very similar between a product or service, but the manner in which we present this proof will vary. Intangible selling of services often requires proof that cannot be measured because *consultants* are being offered as part of the solution, and it is not always clear to the buyer that the consultants are capable. Spouting off data and statistics or going negative on the competition is less effective than telling a relevant story - hence the use of the anecdote.

What is an Anecdote?

Stories sell. There is something about the emotional connection that happens when a story is well-told. Anecdotes are meant to set the other person at ease while making a point that substantiates a claim or overcomes an objection. The following is a personal adaptation of an example presented by Ford Harding in *Making Rainmakers.*

While working at Lawson Software, I remember one sales call I was on with Michael Faulks, the sales manager for our region. We were sitting around a conference table, when the client started off with, "I've had some bad experiences in my career implementing ERP systems. How can I be sure you're going to be able to deliver what I need in the time frame you specify?" Everyone in the room knew that the deal hung on the answer to this question. I looked at Michael, one of the best rainmakers I know, and he responded with the following story:

When I had only been in business a short time, I made a proposal to a client to implement a wholesale distribution solution based on a very specific set of requirements for a large international distributor. Because of the scope of the international configuration and the increased labor we had to apply, the estimate was greater than we had originally communicated to the client. When I met with the owner of the company, he looked at our cost structure and time frame and asked what it would cost. I told him, and he handed back my proposal. He told me that he would seek to source from another company. I said that we could re-work the estimates by taking a different approach. He stated that he couldn't work with someone who didn't listen to him. I've never forgotten that lesson.

That story, so much more effective than promises or statistics, won the deal and solidified a long-term client. Anecdotes are powerful and can be used to sell anything. They can also be used by individuals to demonstrate their personal resume and offer proof as to why a company should hire them.

Here are some guidelines suggested by Harding:

First, the anecdote must be relevant to the prospect's or client's problem. In the telling, the seller must relate an experience to their

specific skills that created value for a customer. Then they need to pick

the right anecdote that is similar to the challenge the prospect is facing.

Second, the anecdote must confirm the seller's understanding of the

prospect's or client's situation well enough to illustrate that the seller had

previously faced this problem. Just listing several references is less

effective than comparing the prospect's challenge to a well-constructed

anecdote.

Third, the anecdote may be used to probe into an area where a direct

question to the prospect or client may prove to be risky. The anecdote

should allow a seller to test a problem from another client to see if there

is relevance to this particular prospect or client. The anecdote can also

be used to politely tell the prospect or client that he or she is wrong

because the seller has illustrated where the same symptom had a bad

outcome. In this way, you can use the anecdote to narrow the scope so

that a pre-proposal is accurate and consistent with the prospect's or

client's problem.

Finally, the anecdote can be used to demonstrate characteristics unique

to the seller's firm, that would persuade the prospect or client to choose

the seller's organization to solve their problem. You can share an

experience that highlights a cultural or behavioral quality that would

endear you to the client. Each employee should have a group of

anecdotes that demonstrate his or her skills and background along with examples of how their company has solved a problem for another client.

The reason it is important for the entire company to be able to effectively relate their stories is because like it or not, every employee is in sales. As the seller's company begins to grow their footprint inside of the buyer's organization, the internal connecting expands. One of the skills of a good project manager is to manage by walking around and interact with the client and staff. This behavior should not be limited to managers only; it is vital for every consultant on the project to interact with the client and staff. As a client's staff begins to ask members of the implementation team questions about their other capabilities, the answers should be consistent and based on an anecdote. In this way, an implementation team will tell stories about an existing solution, which will lead to increased interest. Often the most credible employees at a seller's company are those who are not in direct sales and never have been. For example, we know that in a technical sale, technicians would rather buy from other technicians instead of having a salesperson as a middleman. Dipesh (mentioned previously in chapter 4) would say that as he started building his company, telling stories about different engagements where he had solved similar challenges became his secret sauce. He had thought through which stories had the most relevance to

the prospective client with whom he was currently engaged. In sum, the effective use of stories helped to launch his company.

I remember when I met Dipesh as a young consultant. He had come to Pariveda Solutions after a stint at Deloitte Consulting. He was confident and passionate, and yet he considered himself an introvert. As he began to embrace the notion of networking for life, he decided to be one of the campus champions at The University of Texas, where the company recruited heavily and from where he had graduated. For Dipesh, it was a non-threatening environment to gain experience in networking. He traveled to UT regularly and honed his storytelling skills where he compared a large firm (like Deloitte) to a smaller firm (like Pariveda). I remember one trip we took to Austin together where we had a few prospective students who were being heavily recruited by larger consulting firms. When Dipesh related to them the experience they would receive by being on the front lines at a smaller firm, they were sold. Because he had credibility and experience, they chose to go to work at Pariveda Solutions instead of the larger firms that were recruiting on campus. Pariveda benefited from this intangible sale by recruiting quality individuals. Having closed his first sale, Dipesh built on that confidence over the years until he started his own business (see Chapter 4). What an accomplishment!

The Structure of an Anecdote

In addition to the story being relevant, the characters in the story must also be relatable to the listener. There are four basic components to a good anecdote: a ***plot, a character, an action, and an outcome.***

- The ***Plot*** is built around the fundamental threat or opportunity that the character in the story will face. This might be an increasingly strong competitor who is gaining market share, or a new technology that is disrupting a market. There can only be one plot per anecdote.

- The ***Character*** of the story must give the prospective client someone with whom the client can identify. The character also increases the value of the story. Often, tellers leave the character out of the story – which is a mistake. People will better identify with individuals who have faced similar situations. This is part of an emotional connection.

- ***Action*** creates interest as visual images are described for the listener. These images conveyed by the teller, can anchor the listener and elicit emotion which connects the listener to the story.

- A good story has a desired ***Outcome***. Never leave the listener to figure out for themselves what happened in the story. The teller

must control the takeaway from the anecdote, because if you don't, the listener may come to the wrong conclusion.

- Finally, it must be brief. A good anecdote is five or six sentences, excluding positioning statements.

Here is an example from Harding's book told by an attorney seeking to caution clients that they may not have the best approach for turning over their estate to their children. The story tactfully shows the client that they may be wrong. Then, it educates them, and shows the value of the lawyer's experience, which helps make the sale.

"Not long ago I had a meeting like several others I have had in the past. An elderly couple had put their life into their business, and the children had come to work there. When the couple wanted to retire, they wanted to sell it to the children. All the parents wanted was enough money for their retirement. The business was valued, stock issued, and the parents were given a share of the stock, which provided the income they needed for their retirement. They moved to Boca Raton, enjoyed their retirement, and grew older. Then the business took a hard turn, and the children ended up having to close and liquidate it. There was nothing left for the parents because they hadn't protected themselves against this eventuality. It didn't help that the closure wasn't really the children's fault."

Components

- *Plot:* An elderly couple needs to transfer their business in a way that gives them funds for retirement and provides their children employment.

- *Character:* An elderly couple that the listener, also an elderly person, can identify with.

- *Action:* Moving to Florida. Liquidating the business.

- *Outcome:* The elderly couple left without money.

Once the pattern has been established at the seller's company, anecdotes can be used to address different kinds of problems. They can be used to demonstrate a specific problem solved for a client or substantiate the capabilities of the firm. Anecdotes can also be used to demonstrate individual problem-solving skills or technical expertise. In Dipesh's instance, the anecdote was the impetus for hiring a new employee. Integrating the use of anecdotes in a technical firm should lead to increased selling success.

Chapter 11 - Organizational Power Maps

Now that you have selected stories relevant to the account, it is time to focus on the complexity of the organization with which you are engaged. Every company is a living and breathing entity with culture, norms, taboos, and dysfunctions from top to bottom. I often remind young consultants that they should not complain about the challenges they see in a particular company because it is that challenge that provides consultants with an income. In more complex companies, I recommend that consultants map the organization so that they understand formal and informal structures, budgets, and what is on the mind of the senior executives. Consider the various skills you have been learning as building a base of connecting habits. When these habits are applied to your business and/or personal life, they can lead to success. The reason we are targeting consultancies in this chapter is that the vast majority of consultants are delivering work at a client's location. Over my entire career, I have heard the debate between delivery people and sales-leaning people about who creates more value for the firm. The goal of this book is to show that both are important and vital. However, it may be easier for a technical delivery professional to learn sales skills than for a sales professional to become deeply technical. The key to learning this concept is to acknowledge that it is not just about delivering quality work,

but rather, understanding how an organization makes decisions. The larger the company, the more competitive it is because big companies are big targets for big consultancies. If you are a smaller consultancy, carve out an easier territory to defend or become very good at executing the concepts in Connect for Life. Even as you are delivering the work, some other party, internal or external, is working on displacing you or your company. It is a daily battle of gaining mind share, creating opportunities, and delivering quality. It is not enough to deliver quality if nobody knows how well you are doing. Understanding an organization's nuances are critical to delivering quality work over an extended period of time.

Turning a single engagement into a "flywheel" account over time needs every member of the team to be a true connector inside of the client firm. Where is the power inside of a company? Who has worked with whom in the past? What are the formal versus informal networks? How do I figure it out? How do I balance my effort between delivering quality work, managing people, and mapping out the organizational structure of the business?

It takes effort. If you are at a client's site every day, there is no excuse for lacking the understanding of how an organization makes decisions. Assign every member of the team to a discovery area, and then meet weekly and share what everyone has learned. If one is selling

into the organization for the first time, it can be more complex. In either case, one must know where the power is inside the enterprise. What do we mean by power? Power people control things such as strategy, budget, resources, contracts, time frame, and every other aspect of delivering value to the enterprise. What makes it difficult is that it is not always clear who is really in charge of what. Harold Geneen, the controversial businessman and former CEO of ITT said, "Every company has two organizational structures: The formal one is written on the charts; the other is the living relationship of the men and women in the organization."

As a connector, one must penetrate both structures. Often the word *power* is associated with individuals, but more often power is about the politics of an organization. The politics are the way that a company makes decisions, whether functional or dysfunctional. Power and politics go together, and as a connector, one must understand where the power resides, how to recognize it, how to create it, and how to trade for it if one is going to be successful. Power is often invisible and dynamic. It changes regularly--often daily or weekly--so the account strategy needs to understand the nuances of these relationships.

Rick Page, in *Hope is Not a Strategy,* points out that in some cases, there are votes you "don't want to get" because their support of your solution will alienate others inside the organization. I have seen this

play out time after time where a seller overestimates the power of an individual because they have a title. Because that title is historically associated with being a decision maker, the seller puts all their effort into that one person, and sometimes they lose. For example, there is a trend in many organizations where a business unit hires technical consultants or employees outside of the information technology (IT) organization. The industry often refers to that type of organization as a shadow IT organization because they are not using IT to do a project.

Many companies today are unhappy with the level of service they get from internal IT, so they take the responsibility and solve their own challenges without the IT department. Many sellers look to a CIO as an entry point to the company, however, an organization that has a lot of shadow IT may be dissatisfied with their CIO. Two factors you need to consider are the presence of shadow IT and whether the CIO reports to the chief financial officer (CFO). If the CFO controls the CIO and the budget you might want to reconsider this as an entry point. If one aligns with the CIO without understanding the dynamic of the organization, one might get his or her vote, but as IT starts to promote your organization or solution, credibility suffers.

Hope is Not a Strategy points out four things you need to know about power:

1. You need to know how to identify power and who has it inside the account. Your strategy should then allocate time to those people and secure their support.

2. If one does not have power, it can be borrowed. Leveraging the power of one company executive to get to another is a good strategy.

3. You need to spend time building an internal network of influence inside the company to help get things done or break down barriers.

Executing an internal strategy is not always easy and it must always be done with finesse. Do not make the mistake of forcing access to power. Also, never underestimate the roots of relationships that go back for years. Most of the time, you will learn who has power and then negotiate access to power.

One line of questioning, taken from a similar situation in *Solution Selling*, might go like this:

> "Tom, let's say it is possible to streamline the supply chain, offer you an effective ecommerce solution, link you directly to your wholesaler and lower your operation cost and risk and, you

become convinced that we are the right company to help you deliver? Once you say "yes," what has to happen next?"

There are only two answers according to *Solution Selling*:

1. "I'll buy it. It's my decision and I have the budget and will sign your engagement letter. "

   (Frankly, this one makes me nervous because of politics. A solution as broad as this touches many fiefdoms inside of a company, and while they may be able to sign an engagement letter, the implementation may be a failure. Remember, people support what they help to create.)

2. "I would have to take it to (name of committee or specific person)."

   (Hopefully, your organizational understanding has revealed who that person is. Otherwise, try to get the buyer to reveal who that person is and see if you can negotiate access)

At this point, you put forth the first test:

"Tom, since I'm here, may I meet him today?"

"No, it's too early. Mike, I want to first be convinced that what you say is really feasible."

(This is normal, don't panic! If your buyer wasn't going to give up access to power, it is better to understand it sooner rather than later. With understanding, one can develop some strategies on

how to move forward. But now one has a chit. A chit is

something of value because one has respected a person or

process. In negotiating access to power, a chit is a favor that you

can use later to negotiate a meeting or introduction)

Now, using ideas from Bosworth's *Solution Selling,* it is time to negotiate.

"Would you be willing to make an agreement with me? I'm not

yet sure the best way to prove both our capabilities and the value

of what we have to offer. Whatever that method, it will require an

investment by my company of money, resources, and time. As a

steward of our company's assets, I'm held accountable for using

those resources wisely. We are willing to make that commitment

today. If we succeed in delivering proof that we can (restate

buyers vision), will you introduce me to (power person)? Is that

fair?"

A small percentage of people will not bargain, but they will almost always

agree that the proposed bargain is fair. When an individual will not

provide access to power, there is usually one reason, political fear. It

may be reorganization, a new boss, the company is for sale, numbers

are down, or the last time they took something upstairs they got shot

down. Sometimes, when you do not get to a power person, it is because

the person you are talking to has less power than they think. If they are

savvy, they will leverage your expertise to learn something about their company that would help their career.

I have experienced both types of blockers, ones with power and those who thought they had power but did not. In the latter example, I was working with an IT director who wanted to get deeper into the details before she "allowed" our firm to move around in the organization. If someone on my team spoke to anybody outside of her organization, I would hear about it. In this situation, never go around this type of person because they will see that you don't continue working at the company. Work diligently under that structure and slowly make friends with other executives. Over time, they will figure out that you have something to offer.

In contrast, I was working with a CIO who gave me complete access to power. In the first meeting at the company I asked him to have all of the C-level folks in attendance and when we showed up, they were there. (Side note, you better be prepared for this type of success because you will not get a second chance.) During the meeting, I defined a series of steps we would go through to determine if we were a good fit. We would interview a number of people and report back to this steering committee. Then, we could decide together the best way forward. The process allowed me to understand the organization at a depth such that our pitch was solid, and we won the account. What I didn't find out until

years later, was that the CIO had the intention of being the CEO of the company someday, and he used my skills in mapping organization power to his advantage. In the end, he used me to advance his career. Not in a bad way, but in a way that helped him to deliver incremental value to the organization. Years later, he was CEO. In the end, one must be astute, smart, flexible, and patient. Bosworth postulates that the best way to proceed here is with empathy:

> "I understand the situation. It sounds like this might be tough for you at this time. Since you agree that this solution will benefit you personally and the organization as a whole, could you suggest someone else I might call, who if they see the same value, may be willing to take this upstairs?"

Gaining and negotiating access to power is difficult and requires patience, empathy, and skill. If you push too hard, you may find yourself out on the street. Also, *never* overestimate a relationship that you have with a power person at a client organization.

Think about what it takes for an executive to be successful in today's complex environment. It is not surprising to find them surrounded by individuals who are loyal to them and have provided very important service for them over time. Often, they have worked together before, so their communication is less formal and often behind the scenes. Factoring in this possibility is very important to know where you stand

before a calculated move can be made. When you cross a long-term relationship, the future is not bright for delivering services in that organization. You might begin an engagement, but that person who was crossed will accelerate the organizational antibodies and they will eventually kill your project.

Power Map

One of the tools that we use in account planning is the power map. This tool illustrates how the shadow organization may be driving policy at the company. Outlining the organization using colors provides a quick perspective on who is supporting your firm (green), who is against your firm or supports another company (red), and who is neutral and can be influenced to green (yellow). A power map should drive activities in your account strategy.

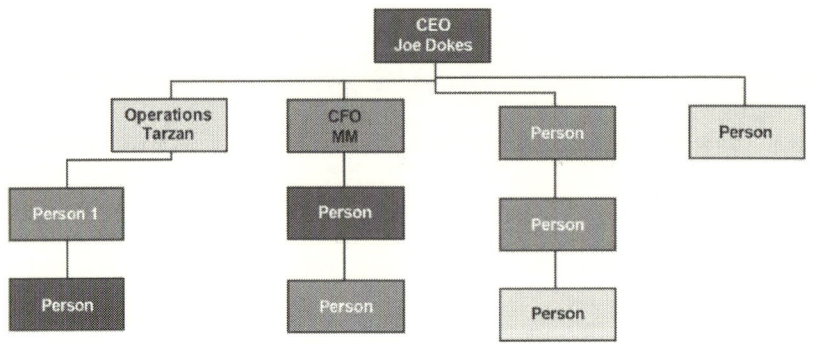

When I was a less experienced connector I had the opportunity to learn how to penetrate and manage an account from a very experienced connector. In his focus market he had skillfully mapped

most of the Fortune 500 companies. Each day he started by looking at what progress he had made in the account. Each day he created a small plan to influence the organizational power to support his products and services. Because of this process, he was able to isolate those who did not favor his company and he created fear, uncertainty, and doubt (FUD) about the solutions those people were suggesting. He fed that information to his supporters and they solidified that point of view in the company. While subtle, this approach empowers the people who support you in the organization with the knowledge of the different approaches the company might take with a bias toward or against you or your solution. In his best year, he sold over $30 million in software to the Fortune 500. It is amazing what happens when one regularly writes down what they learn about the company in this tool. It works.

There are many other influencers that one should be aware of, both positive and negative, legal and illegal. While our integrity prohibits us from doing anything illegal, one might be facing a competitor who has a bad moral compass.

- Tenure, seniority
- Mentors
- Shared experiences
- Threats, intimidation
- Control of resources
- Common friends
- Ethics, fairness
- Teams
- Previous work

- Who hired whom
- Family
- Dependability
- Humor
- Vision
- Tradition, culture
- Connections
- Information
- Credentials

Solution Selling

As you explore the answers to the above personnel intersections, you will uncover critical information that will help in discovering organizational power. Once you understand the power structure, a winning strategy may be created. Using the power map creates a visual representation of the organization and will provide insight that might otherwise be overlooked.

Every pursuit involves developing champions to the cause you are selling. The first objective is understanding the power structure and then working to develop a sponsor or coach based on that understanding. Developing a coach is critical to winning. A coach is someone who believes in the approach being presented and they are willing to help navigate the complexities of the organization. A real coach shows trust when they are revealing information to you that they are not revealing to others. One of the biggest mistakes inexperienced

connectors make is believing they have a coach when they do not. It is important to ask the question, "What are they telling me that they are not telling others?" That is the acid test.

Building influence, in an ethical manner, is the cornerstone of a relationship which in turn evolves into trust when tested. Theodore Levitt, in his book *Thinking About Management,* says it well:

> Trust and reputation are not discretionary. They have always been necessary for doing business, and increasingly so as those who deal with each other are strangers and live distantly from each other.
>
> Often they appear casually social, convivially involving play, food, drink and spouses. In fact, they are anything but casual. The rituals are fixed and taken seriously by their participants. Their purposes are clear but unspoken – to test one another's veracity, reliability, and trustworthiness, to create and reciprocate obligations of performance, and to ascertain via close observance in casual settings the extent to which claims and promises that cannot be tested in advance can be relied upon, lest terrible consequences follow later.

Another great tool used for understanding organizational power is outlined in Page's book, *Hope is Not a Strategy*, which he calls Food Chain of Value or "The Shark Chart".

> *This illustration in the book <u>Hope is Not a Strategy</u>, depicts how bigger issues tend to eat up smaller ones. The "C" Suite is focused on strategic ideas and they live above the dotted line. Not only do they care less about operational issues, they often veto those projects as they bubble up even after both their company and their vendors have invested considerable time. Understanding this dynamic both from a requirement, pain and a political perspective is important to finding the true challenges of the organization and creating a winning value proposition.*

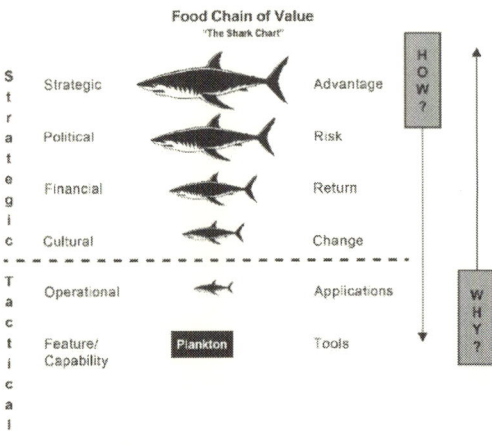

Once the organization has been mapped, an understanding should develop between what is considered tactical versus strategic. Through connections, those who support your approach will tell you what is important, who is responsible, and the best way to approach that individual. Exerting organizational influence is key and one does that through being authentic and trustworthy, not by using deception or trickery. Influence is the process whereby an individual gets things done through other people without the use of authority. The use of moral persuasion is used on projects every day to meet deadlines and manage people. The same is true in selling. The key is determining who has real influence at our accounts and who does not. Individuals can have

influence with no authority, or they can have authority, but no influence. There are people with both and those with neither. The challenge is figuring out this puzzle as it is the key to organizational selling, and it takes time. If you are not investing your time appropriately in the account, you will not learn what you need to know to deliver value. Many of these methods are useful depending on the size and complexity of the client. If one is pursuing a large company, it applies 100%. If one is pursuing a small to mid-sized company, this type of methodology is overkill because you are probably talking to the owner or president.

Power is another word for position, influence, budget, or control. Every time a sales cycle is launched talking to a low-level person about your product or service, you put the deal at risk. It's as if you are saying, *"Take all of the information that I have given you, filter it, edit it, and then pass it on to your boss when you think it is appropriate."* It sounds funny when written down, but this happens to sellers every day. Focus on the power in the firm you are trying to penetrate. Beware of how power is characterized because the larger the firm, the more people who believe they have power. Be careful not to blow off director-level individuals who have power even if they do not have the C-level title as you will lose.

Networking through the organization and mapping it accordingly is critical. If you do not map it correctly, your company loses. If you take

the stewardship of your firm's resources seriously and if you want to

advance your career, this effort leads to success.

Chapter 12 - Selling Between the Lines

If we evaluate an organization in the context of how an economy grows, an economy is simply a place where capital is allocated to get the best return. It is amazing how it works as dollars flow where they can create more dollars. An organization operates in a similar fashion. I remember the first economics class I had at Southern Methodist University (SMU) where the professor spent a lot of time talking about marginal utility, which is economic jargon for the benefit one derives by doing various activities. The professor would consistently tie economic models back to the utility that various activities created for the individual or the company. One of the wonderful characteristics of a free economy is that each day the participants decide for themselves what they want to do and how much they want to spend. No other individual or central planner can decide what is best for an individual. Choice is the cornerstone of a free economy, and we take part in that economy by consuming and saving based on what gives us the greatest utility. That utility is not just dollars and cents, but the things in life from which one derives joy and happiness. In theory, a company is a collection of like-minded people working toward a common goal by efficiently allocating available capital.

A corporation's job is to create a return for the people who own the company and for the employees who work there. Regardless of

whether a company is publicly or privately held, the return for that enterprise is to the owner or owners. The hierarchy of a company typically follows this structure: the shareholders vote for a slate of directors on the Board, elects a chairman, and then the Board hires the chief executive officer. The CEO is the senior most executive responsible for the performance of the company and is charged with generating returns for shareholders. If you consider that a Fortune 5000 company is a microcosm of the broader economy, where scarce resources are allocated efficiently, executives should behave similarly. Notwithstanding the many poor decisions companies make, executives are usually operating to the best of their ability and focused on generating a return. A return is defined as getting more back than you invest. This important fundamental shows how companies make money. As a connector, the economic activity we are reviewing in this chapter links the work you are doing or selling with the economic viability of an organization. Let's back up for a moment. Why is a person engaged in this enterprise in the first place? It seems as if the answer has an obvious reason, but there is an internal one as well, a reason that resonates in the soul. On the surface, we are working hard to create value for our families, provide choices for where to live and go to school and what leisure activities we might enjoy. Internally, we are also looking for respect and significance. We desire to engage in those activities that matter and create value. If that is

accomplished, we will be recognized for the value they have created. Organizations are not that dissimilar from individuals. They want to provide a return for shareholders, a good place for people to make a living, and for the most part, they want to do things that matter. As you begin to dig into those areas between the lines, it is important to quantify the value being created for the enterprise.

There are four basic inputs that need to be understood in the context of a solution. Every seller's product or service needs to be linked to how those solutions will increase revenue, improve gross profit, lower indirect costs, or manage business risk. This is called selling between the lines. The metaphor is derived from the look of a profit and loss statement (P&L), which starts at the top with revenue. Revenue is the top line aggregation of all the sales that flow into the company. The next line is cost of goods sold (COGS), which is the cost of the inputs necessary to create the products and services a company is selling. Revenue minus cost of goods sold equals gross profit. Gross profit is the line from which everything else is deducted. When a CFO refers to monies above the line, they are typically referring to COGS. The most important number, referred to as the bottom line, is net income --the money left over after everything is spent, including taxes. Overlaying all of the input lines in a P&L is managing the risk of a business to ensure the company is hedged against the inevitability of a negative exogenous event. Thus, selling

between the lines should be a focus for every seller. Every offering one sells should be positioned in terms of these four measures – revenue, cost of goods sold, net income, and business risk.

Revenue – Is your offering going to help drive sales for the customer? In other words, is your idea for the company going to drive top line growth through acquisition of new clients or access to new markets? How about gaining a larger share of wallet from existing clients? When Apple created the iPod and iTunes it generated huge top-line growth for the company, and it also drove sales for record labels and artists who were under assault from individuals stealing music through websites like Napster. Apple made it so easy and the user experience was so awesome, it was viewed by customers as being better than free. Today, companies and markets are being disrupted in full view of the world. Just look at the retail business, for example, and how retailers are combating being "Amazoned." Does your firm have an offering that will help these companies? Because if they do not change, they will cease to exist.

Cost of Goods Sold (COGS) – Is your offering helping to improve the customer's gross profit by lowering COGS? If you have an offering that will lower cost of goods sold and improve gross profit, you have a home run. Maybe you are an engineering company and your manufacturing process turns raw material into finished goods faster and cheaper. Maybe you have technology that will speed up the entire supply

chain so you can be the low-cost producer. Consider the huge jump that Ford Motor Company made by building its 2016 pickup trucks with an aluminum frame. Think of all of the work that Ford needed to do with their suppliers and all of the hoops that were necessary to jump through in order to configure an end-to-end supply chain for aluminum chassis. This was a very complex sale, both internally for Ford and for all the participants in the supply chain.

Back in 1999, I was working on selling enterprise software in the wholesale distribution market. One of the issues that a president of a large company told me was concerning the need to enforce the pricing policies of the company's trading operation. If he could enforce the pricing that was set by the head trader, the other traders could not give away product at lower prices. This was a core piece of functionality that our system ensured, and so we tied a value proposition to improved gross margin that the company attributed to that specific functionality. As I recall, our demonstrations were limited to the 3 or 4 features that led to real return. We did not demonstrate anything else, and the entire demo took about an hour. We ultimately won the engagement.

Net Income –Will your offering lower general operating costs for the business and increase the company's net income? As companies are always looking at how they can be more efficient, lowering selling, general, and administrative costs (SG&A) is critical. For years, Walmart

deployed technology, people, and processes to create the most efficient supply chain in the world. These investments lowered Walmart's costs of doing business so they could deliver less costly products to stores and become THE low-cost producer. Along comes Amazon and wham! Walmart got "Amazoned." In another instance, we built an online trading platform for a trading operation. Because we created an intuitive online experience, the system attracted more users, which drove top line sales. The solution also increased the share of wallet (more of their internal spend went to the distributor) from existing clients which led to a growth in sales. Since clients could trade in real-time (24 hours a day) the company was able to take more trades per hour than their trading operation could prior to implementing the online platform. Finally, because the cost of trading declined, the company was able to do more with fewer people and this freed up the trading operation to sell higher-margin products to its customers. The system also freed up trader's time, enabling them to make outbound sales calls which led to increased revenue. That solution was a home run because it addressed almost every dimension in the between the lines model!

Business Risk – Is your offering lowering the customer's general business risk? Thinking about risk goes beyond the assets that a company insures. Consider other types of events--economic, atmospheric, geopolitical, pandemic--that could seriously damage an

enterprise if those events came to fruition. There is great lore about the early days at PayPal when the company was creating a disrupting payment infrastructure. In his book, *Zero to One,* Peter Thiel, one of the founders of PayPal, mentions that at one point the company was losing close to $10 million per month in fraudulent transactions. PayPal's engineers thought they could create an artificial intelligence platform that could eliminate the fraud, but it didn't work. It wasn't until the company put analysts in charge of reviewing the data in real time, that PayPal was able to create a solution and identify the fraud before additional losses were incurred. The analysts could see patterns that the software could not. The company was so successful at eliminating this risk from the business that the FBI licensed the technology and processes from PayPal. In another example, a good friend of mine owned a manufacturing company in Fort Worth, which he sold. He financed the sale with the company's stock as collateral. The buyer ran the company into the ground, and in a board meeting my friend challenged the CFO by asking if all the company's insurance policies were still in place. My friend stated, "what this firm needs is a good disaster." He was joking of course about the disaster, but not about the insurance policies in a company that was struggling financially. Three days later a tornado hit Fort Worth and destroyed the facility. He repossessed the company and

reopened at a new location. Risks to businesses are real and not always easily foreseen.

No matter what you are selling, going through the exercise of evaluating how your offerings create value between the lines is critical. By writing down the opportunities, you can begin to assemble the anecdotes from real client examples that support the value proposition that you are offering. In this way, good sellers connect solutions to value and deploy those solutions to the appropriate clients. Good connectors are not slick; they are prepared, and they do their homework.

In covering selling between the lines after a chapter on power maps, we link the concept of value creation to the understanding of the power within an organization. Only by penetrating and connecting throughout the organization, can a person discover the opportunities and the inputs necessary to develop a return on investment (ROI) calculation. Without real numbers that can be supported and validated by somebody in the organization, the ROI will get shot down. I have seen this strategy play out year after year, not only in the consulting industry but also in many other service industries. This strategy is very simple: target the right companies who need services around your core competency, do great work, and measure your success. While doing these activities, you need to constantly be connecting and penetrating further into an account and seeking new opportunities. If you or your firm delivers quality work,

you should never be hesitant to ask the client for the opportunity to propose on other projects.

Several years into the journey at Pariveda Solutions, I helped a talented person join the firm as vice president in the Dallas office. One of his challenges came from not being trained in traditional consulting so he struggled with estimating projects, managing a team, and growing people. His greatest skill was connecting with people and selling. He was a great student of the *Connect for Life* methodology, and he was particularly astute at valuing work in the context of what the client thought was the most important thing. He sold between the lines every day and was able to craft creative solutions and achieve trusted advisor status.

Some consulting firms tend to be a little self-righteous about where an individual started their career. If a career began at Deloitte or Accenture, or one of the top firms like Booze Allen Hamilton, then a newly hired consultant is accepted more readily. But if you are from the outside, you will have to prove yourself. As the vice president in our Dallas Pariveda office grew his skills in consulting he landed a new account at a billion-dollar privately held services company. Over the next couple years, he grew the team from three consultants to over twenty-seven consultants and had a run rate of revenue in the millions of dollars. His team delivered over and over, and this VP came to know all

of the executives and worked through challenges, opportunities, and issues with the client's success in mind. He consistently did his homework and mapped his position across the firm. He knew the strategy of the firm, and his team became a great conduit for new ideas regarding where value was being created, and where value might be created in the future. This is an example of how connecting starts small with little wins, and over time creates a trusted advisor relationship. This in turn raises one's stature inside a client company from being a vendor to becoming a trusted partner. This individual has since parlayed that experience into starting his own firm and achieved extraordinary success.

I'm not giving you examples of people who have excelled at connecting and networking to illustrate how you can start your own company, although that is possible. I'm trying to encourage you to follow some basic processes and principles that will enable you to become a better creator of value for your clients. The more this is accomplished, the more successful you will be, becoming more valuable to your clients and ultimately your employer.

Chapter 13 – Tools for Preparation

Have a Global Perspective

External forces, internal forces, and potential exogenous events all affect the modern-day enterprise; therefore, anyone developing relationships in a Fortune 500 company needs to have context of the global economy. Every day, executives look at where their company is in an economic cycle as a barometer of where they should or should not invest, and how they should direct their employees. As I mentioned in the previous chapter, it is important to understand the cycle between the lines because the profitability of a company changes based upon an economic cycle. Without diverging too far into an economic discussion, you should be able to speak intelligently about general market conditions and develop a point of view. Today, the media is powerful in its messaging; however, as an advisor, you need to establish your own opinion based on research and facts. Having a global context derived from reading, researching, and talking with others is critical. Do not just repeat what the pundits are saying on television; develop your own point of view.

In his book, *Get Rich Carefully,* Jim Cramer advises the reader to listen to the quarterly conference calls of companies Caterpillar(CAT) and Alcoa to get a feel for economic conditions in Asia. Because of the material that Alcoa provides to the airline industry, their earnings are also

a proxy for Boeing's backlog in manufacturing. Cramer recommends

listening to the United Technologies quarterly conference calls to gauge

how commercial real estate is faring. Walt Disney should be explored to

get a pulse on the consumer. Toll Brothers and Home Depot should be

scrutinized for the current condition of home building. This is a brilliant

strategy because one is getting to the source of the data without listening

to TV personalities who have filtered the material to sell advertising. The

topic of a value chain is covered in the next section, but by

understanding the manufacturing cycle from raw materials through

production and sales, one can execute Cramer's strategy. If

infrastructure growth is robust in China, CAT will have a large number of

backorders for heavy equipment and revenue will be robust. If Alcoa is

booming, Boeing and Airbus are buying aluminum and growing. United

Technologies is the largest manufacturer of elevators in the world,

serving as a barometer for the global commercial real estate market.

Because economic growth is all about the consumer (more to come),

Walt Disney has a broad view of how the consumer is actually spending

their money. And finally, because residential real estate is typically the

largest asset owned by a family, Toll Brothers and Home Depot will

create a picture of where the consumer is in making or enhancing their

most valuable asset. By listening directly to the analysis reported by

these leading public companies, you will gain a broader context on the

economy both domestically and abroad. Understanding both the economic cycle and global economic conditions will enable you to direct the team to opportunities and give insight as to what is on the minds of the executives of the company that you are targeting.

This strategy for developing an economic point of view is not only creative, but it also leads to better understanding of what is really going on in a segment of the economy. Executives are actively directing the allocation of capital and resources based on what they think they will sell and produce in the next 12 to 18 months. Then they get on a conference call and tell the world the current forecast for their business and what they are planning. Beware of listening to economists who have never run a business; instead, listen to the CEO at CAT describe his current strategy for Asia, which has far more credibility. United Technologies will describe their forecast of demand and that will tell us about who is building buildings and where those projects are located. When Walt Disney discusses head count and traffic at its amusement parks and retail operations, you will get a sense of how the consumer is spending their money. This knowledge makes one conversational. Imagine being in an executive meeting at a company in retail and being able to add context to a discussion by adding, "Last night I listened to the Disney conference call and they indicated this or that." The first thing that the executive might realize is that he did not listen to the call, nor did

anyone on his team. The next thing he might do is ask you a question

about the call, thus elevating your status from vendor to trusted advisor.

Know the Market Cycle

Next, it is important to understand market cycles. Harvard Professor

Joseph Ellis has written a very practical book, *Ahead of the Curve.* This

book outlines the basic inputs and outputs of an economy, and how the

rates of change in a particular facet of the economy affect the consumer.

In the diagram below, we see the growth engine of an economy is real

consumer spending. Most economists, including Ellis, agree that as the

consumer goes, so goes the economy. In the United States, consumer

spending accounts for 70% of gross domestic product (GDP).

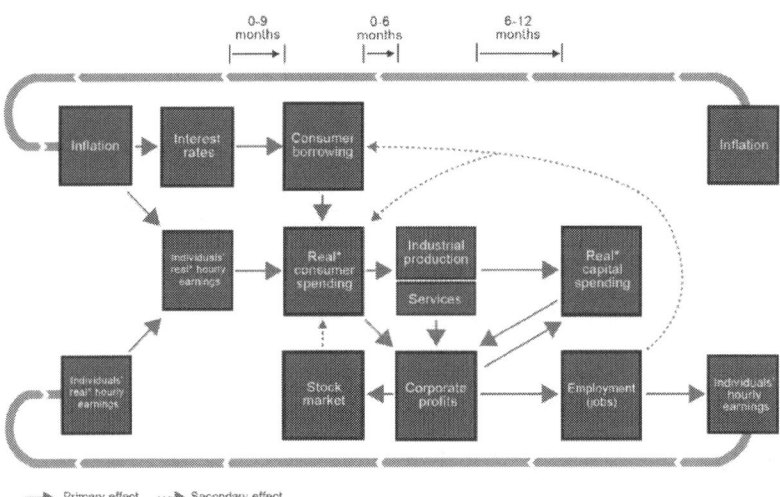

Joseph Ellis – _Ahead of the Curve_

The baby boomer generation that moved through the economy for the last 50 years has affected every segment of our economy. When their parents came back from WWII, they bought houses. As the baby boomers came of age, they started raising families and they bought consumables. Today the U.S. boomer consumer is older and spending money on healthcare, assisted living, and travel. These demographics will have an effect on future economic cycles because elderly people tend to spend less money. In China, the government is trying to shift to more of a consumer-based economy from an infrastructure-based economy. When the government is spending on infrastructure like highways, buildings and airports, those investments are funded with debt to pay for materials and worker's wages. The wages that workers receive are used for basic needs. On a relative basis, the economic impact is much greater when the consumer is spending money. When real consumer spending is high it drives industrial production and services, which in turn drives corporate profits and creates jobs, which in turn creates competition for jobs as wages increase, eventually driving inflation. As inflation kicks in, interest rates rise, investments slow, and the consumer retrenches. This virtuous cycle goes around and around in a free market economy. Understanding the cycle outlined by Ellis will help you to ask the right questions when researching a company. The

model also allows you to develop a point of view on tax policy, Federal Reserve policies, or other external policies that affect how an economy progresses through a cycle.

There is a concept in investing called asset allocation where investors assign capital to various market sectors to develop a well-balanced portfolio. Here is a short list of market sectors: consumer discretionary, consumer staples, energy, financial services, healthcare, industrial production, technology, and international. If an economy is emerging from recession, an investor might have a heavier allocation in energy, industrial production, or consumer discretionary. As an economy improves, spending increases and wages rise. If an economy is at the tail end of a growth cycle, an investor might move to more defensive stocks in healthcare or consumer staples because these companies are more resistant to economic downturns. Using the *Ahead of the Curve* model should provide perspective for where the economy is in the cycle. If your customer or prospect is in a sector at the beginning or end of an economic cycle, they will pick one set of projects over another.

By subscribing to investment newsletters such as *Investech, MorningStar* or *Real Vision* and regularly meeting with a variety of chief financial officers, one can develop a perspective and be more conversational. If a prospect is in a counter cyclical business (meaning it moves opposite from the general economy), we discuss timing for

investments and where to allocate capital. Trying to time a market cycle change is a fool's errand but having a general model that helps you in planning capital expenditures is wise. Quoting statistician George Box, "all models are wrong, some are useful."

Preparation Questions

To be prepared, you should conduct research on the industry, the market cycle, and the company. The following is a list of appropriate questions to prepare:

- How is the economy and the company?
  - Where are we in the economic cycle?
  - Where do you think the business is functioning within the cycle? Doing well? Not doing well? Ready to expand?
  - Is your client a cyclical company? Counter-cyclical? Does it matter?
- What geographic region will be in expansion or contraction?
  - Do you know the unemployment rate in the state where the company is located? Is the local economy generally growing for this industry or not? Should you shift your focus from the east coast to the west coast?
  - What about international influences? Asia? Europe? South America?

- What size companies are doing well?
  - Big? Small?
- How fast is the company growing?
  - Faster growth requires more capital, so you might be competing for limited resources
- Is the company currently being disrupted by market changes?
  - How is this company responding to the disruption?
- Is the company profitable and will they spend money on the services that you provide?
  - What is their tolerance for spending? Is this one you should walk away from before too much investment?
- Do you have a good relationship in multiple areas across the firm?
  - If not, how can you begin to develop relationships across the firm?

Remember, every market, every prospect, and every person, is different.

You must understand both the pain points and the opportunities. Think

like the CEO and solve their problems.

Know the Industry and the Company

The third concept for developing a perspective is knowledge of the

industry and the company. Michael Porter, economist and professor at

Harvard University, has said that with 20 hours of preparation, he can

learn more than the CEO of a Fortune 500 company about their

business. While one may not engage in as deep of an analysis as Porter,

the lesson remains true. In order to succeed, one must prepare.

In his book, *How to Become a Rainmaker,* Jeff Fox makes the following
statements:

> *"Ninety percent of all sales calls are won or lost before the sales*
>
> *person sees the customer."*

"Rainmakers never waste a sales call. They always pre-call plan. It is typical for a Rainmaker to spend three hours planning for a twenty-minute sales call. Planning and practicing for two days to two weeks for a single sales call is not uncommon."

Value Chains

One tool for understanding a company is looking at the value chain. Also known as a supply chain, the value chain is established when value is exchanged between market participants. It is the process by which a product goes from its raw material state to the finished product and eventually the end consumer. Along the way, the product is changed, added to, configured, melted, and moved through the process to the next participant in the value chain. Sometimes the value chain participants are inside the company. Often, they are separate companies in various locations. Understanding the market usually breaks down to understanding the industry value chain, where the pain points are for that company in the value chain, and what your company or service can do to solve that pain point.

In the value chain illustration below, a product moves through a linear cycle from participant to participant from raw materials to the consumer.

Just understanding the key components of a prospective client's value chain will create credibility. Sometimes the value chain is much broader and more complex, and the companies are all separate legal entities. All companies are not created equal, nor are they the same. If one can gain an understanding of how value is created for a firm's customer, a hypothesis can be developed to accentuate various opportunities.

From 1993 to 1995 I worked for a company then named Andersen Consulting. Because Andersen bought the commercial banking software company where I worked, I found myself in the financial services industry practice for Andersen. In that role, I was regularly in New York, Chicago, and San Francisco as many of the top banks in the United States were in these cities. At the time, we were in the infancy of the Internet and the foothills of disruption of the financial services industry, particularly banking. I remember a meeting that we

had with Bank of America with a team of our strategy guys in the

financial services group. The team consisted of 2 senior partners and

several very bright consultants. We pitched our point of view on the

future of branch banking, which included a strong migration to an online

experience. It was 1995 and we were dismissed by the bank's

executives. My how things have changed in twenty years. In an article

published in *TheStreet.com* on June 3, 2015, it was written that:

> "Bank of America (BAC) plans to operate smaller branches, and
>
> fewer of them, while focusing instead on expanding less costly
>
> digital options for its customers. Between 2012 and 2014, Bank
>
> of America reduced the number of branches 11% to 4,855 and
>
> trimmed its full-time workforce 17% to 68,537. While the
>
> Charlotte, N.C.-based bank does plan to expand its presence in
>
> some key markets, Dean Athanasia, the president of preferred
>
> and small business banking and co-head of consumer banking,
>
> said the company wants to double the number of digital
>
> transactions per day -- including deposits made via mobile
>
> devices, which already total $3 billion."

Sometimes you can be right but have the wrong timing. A year or so after

the meeting that the Andersen team had with the Bank of America, BOA

started to execute their online strategy. For years, they downplayed the

cannibalization of their branch network by the online business because

the technology was taking jobs away from the economy and that made BOA a target for negative press.

In this value chain, the retail consumer is demanding a world-class experience online from their financial institutions. The disruption is happening to this value chain in real time, and one can conclude from the above quote that the bank is in a phase of disruption because of changing consumer preferences.

Using this model will allow you to engage in a discussion with your client about where value is being exchanged, and where the market is pulling or pushing the company. One thing is for sure, if a company remains status quo and refuses to change, the company will cease to exist sometime in the future. Just look at Blockbuster, Barnes & Noble, and Kodak – to name a few. Some companies are forced to change because of consumer demand, while others create completely new disruptive ideas and embrace change. Think about the publishing industry going digital, or what Uber has done to taxi services, or what Airbnb is doing to the hotel industry. Uber and Airbnb are completely new and disruptive ideas that were born out of the concept of a shared economy. Both have been tremendously successful and extraordinarily disruptive, and they do not own the assets that generate their revenue.

By understanding a company's internal or external value chain before the first meeting, one will significantly increase their probability of

success. It also helps to understand if the company is a disrupter or is being disrupted. Companies being disrupted are very open to ideas on how they can compete more effectively. It is like selling into the white space that the client can't entirely see because nobody has shown them what is possible. It is difficult to sell into the unknown areas of a business without having a detailed understanding of how that business creates value for its customers.

One of the reasons I worked with a wholesale distributor of precious metals was that the industry was in the middle of disruptive forces where wholesale distributors were buying online retailers, thus vertically integrating the value chain, i.e., they own all the participants in the value chain. The subtlety is that these companies are now competing with their customers. Because my prospect had a forty-year history working directly with retailers, from the small mom-and-pop dealer to the largest banks in the world, they did not want to compete against their customers. If you choose not to compete against your clients, the only choice left is to help them. To accomplish this directive, we created multiple platforms to assist those clients in trading, eCommerce, and in-store solutions. The result was an increase in new customers, an increase in the share of wallet for existing customers, and an increase in customer loyalty. It is not entirely clear how the industry consolidation will affect the roles that companies will play in the value chain, but this client

has created a focused strategy to deal with the challenge. If I had not been an active networker in the marketplace, I would never have received the phone call for an initial lunch with their CFO. This is a perfect example about why it is important to stay connected and think about changes occurring in an industry.

Once a model is developed, you can begin the process of making initial contact or broadening your connections throughout the firm or in a marketplace. Either way, prepare a pre-call checklist. In some cases this can be done formally, while in other cases it can be accomplished before a networking meeting. The idea is to do your homework and be prepared.

Below is an account checklist that will ensure preparedness:

Account Checklist
1. Written objective
    a. What do we want out of this meeting?
    b. Is this a problem you have solved before?
2. Understanding the basic metrics of the company between the lines
    a. Revenue, profit, growth, mergers, divestitures, employees, industry
    b. Public versus private – recent press releases, partnerships, publicly available information
    c. Strengths – What do they do very well?
    d. Weaknesses – Where are their soft spots?
    e. Opportunities – What new business, product or operational ideas can yield benefit to the business?
    f. Threats – What is your view of the competition? Who do they fear and respect?
3. Perspective on the industry
    a. What is disrupting the industry today?
    b. Who are the major players?
    c. Is there disruption coming?
    d. Where is value creation happening in their supply chain?
4. Relationships in the company
    a. Who do you know?
    b. Who do you know who knows them?
    c. What are the next steps from a relationship perspective?
5. Anticipated questions they might ask you.
    a. What might they want to know about your firm?
    b. What concerns might they have?
    c. What do we know about the competition?
6. Establish open-ended questions that you might use in the meeting
    a. Tell me more about…
    b. Would you elaborate on…
    c. Give me an example of…

The level of preparedness by the knowledge worker will separate the

trusted advisor from that of a vendor. The goal is to provide you with

necessary tools to ensure confidence and understanding as you engage

with companies. Planning and preparation are the keys to success in

developing a services business. Those who fail to plan, plan to fail!

Chapter 14 – Getting the First Meeting

Getting the first meeting can be a scary process because often we don't know the person with whom we want to meet. It takes preparation and practice. Effective connectors get the first meeting because they are prepared to win, and they practice winning. Having a process to follow translates these ideas into an actionable plan that will guide you in getting the first meeting. This chapter will show you how to create opportunities through multiple sources– your network, your clients, your friends, and the infamous cold call.

Networking

We have already spent an enormous amount of time discussing networking and connecting but have not discussed how your story relates to acquiring a new client. There are several avenues for networking from the informal time with friends and family to the formal business and networking meetings. By rehearsing your story, you will be prepared for any setting. Have a brief list of target accounts memorized so that as you network, those names are top of mind. You never know when you may be introduced to one of your targets at an event. Establish a habit for creating a plan for the following week and then work that plan throughout the week, constantly measuring progress. Networking is enhanced when you know your reference stories by company size,

territory, and capabilities. When we started Pariveda in 2003 we had two employees. We were both active networkers, and one day I got a note on LinkedIn from a CEO of a small company that supplied software to non-profit organizations. The hardest time to sell in a new company is when you are completely aspirational, and there is nothing behind you: no employees, no reference stories, nothing. When in this position, a person must borrow from the past what has formerly been accomplished. In this way, a person is offering proof from prior companies and engagements. In this case, I had been involved in a pursuit at this company before while working for another employer, but we had not won the engagement. The CEO saw that we had started a new company and asked a simple question, "Do you guys do application development?" I replied, "Yes," and moved to schedule a first meeting.

The first meeting was with the company CEO and COO. We had our stories practiced and shared our vision for developing technical talent. Near the end of the conversation the COO asked the question, "There are many application development shops in DFW who already have teams of developers, so why should we go with you?" I paused to consider my response and then said, "That's a great question. At the end of the day, none of those firms have the two of us."

With that we went on to deliver a proposal, and we eventually won the work. I had never used that line before, nor have I used it since

because it sounds arrogant. I was confident that we could deliver, and that we had capable people joining our company in the fall of 2003. When I talked about practicing your rap at the end of Chapter 3, I introduced the idea that your brain would take the knowledge, combine it with the facts, interpret the situation, and the right words would come out. I knew these guys had struggled with a company they had previously chosen and the software was not delivered. They had spent close to a million dollars and did not have a product. We were honest, direct, and had stories from work we had done previously that provided proof that would make them successful. Because of our earlier track record, these clients trusted that we could help them. I cannot say for sure, but I believe the first meeting was born from the respect and reputation that we had developed earlier in our careers.

Tools

The easiest way to get a meeting is through a referral. Many people manage their network using the social media tools described in Chapter 4. However, if you do not manage those contacts, connect with those contacts, and meet with those contacts on a regular basis, using social media is a waste of time. In the previous story, I got a call because I was actively engaged and communicating with the market regarding our start-up. The individuals who knew us and thought we might be able to help them reached out to us first. It went something like, "tell me about your

new company." In most cases referrals will be from somebody in your network who will point you in the right direction or even make an introduction on your behalf. I have found that most people with whom you have a relationship, will be happy to help build your business. I will discuss cold calling later in this chapter, but there is no doubt that executing a networking and connecting strategy will make cold calling less effective. It is all about building a critical mass of meaningful activity.

I was recently in a seminar conducted by Dave Nelsen, president of Dialog – a social networking think tank. His research has found that in LinkedIn only 25% of your first-level relationships respond to a request for an introduction link, followed by 10% of your second-level contacts, and 3% of your third-level contacts. We have defined LinkedIn before as a network of business people. A first-level relationship is somebody that you know and is personally connected to you on LinkedIn. A second-level relationship is somebody who is directly connected to one of your first-level contacts. A third-level contact is directly connected to one of your second-level contacts. LinkedIn shows the level designation when you search for the name of a contact or a company. If I see somebody in your network with whom I would like to meet, I might ask you to make a warm introduction to that person through the tools on LinkedIn. What Nelson is saying is that even with your first-level contacts, only one in four will make a warm introduction and the percentages fall from there.

The point is you need a different referral strategy. Nelson recommends that once you have found the name of the person you want to meet, go outside of LinkedIn and use email, text or phone to get in touch with your first-level contact and ask for an introduction. In other words, connect with someone in your network whom you know well and ask for help. You can send a friendly email to your contact asking for a warm introduction to an executive you are trying to meet. If you are close with this person, you can call or text them.

This brings us to the difference between networking and connecting. Back in Chapter 3, I mentioned the importance of being careful about whom to allow in your first-level connection network because you need to have met that person. If you are just pounding out invites so you can have a large number of connections in your network, then you are actually diluting the value of your social capital as outlined in Chapter 4. More is not better. Better is better.

Nelsen recommends the use of people search on LinkedIn to find people using key words, industries, and other items to educate yourself on the potential targets. My experience is that using Sales Navigator provided by LinkedIn is a critical tool in connecting with others. Former employees are another great source of information. Nelson mentions that those people will often share company challenges, penetration points, and other interesting facts about the people or

account. Remember Harvey Mackay who says you must continuously refresh your network. By staying in touch, your connections will never feel taken advantage of when you are asking for help.

Many of us overlook our existing relationships as a source of warm introductions. To avoid taking advantage of friends, we do not mention business topics during social gatherings or lunches. Rather than look to your friend network as potential prospects, ask them for help with introductions. Most of us underestimate how much those friends want to help us and will if asked. If you are professional and deliver impressive results in the market, why wouldn't they want to do business with you? If you are honest about what you can and cannot do for them, the trust level will remain. Mostly, they just want to help. Other sources of introductions are clients. An existing client who is happy with your work may be willing to get you in front of people in their network. Most executives are involved in several external organizations and as you build your relationship, you can ask for an introduction to one or more of the executive's contacts. Once you have an introduction, plan your strategy, timing, and focus before having those meetings. Being prepared is never more important than when meeting with a lead source from a friend. Always follow-up with your contact who made the introduction and keep them abreast of what is going on. If you don't

follow-up with your friend, you could lose them as a valuable source of warm introductions.

First Impressions

Your mom was right – you never get a second chance to make a good first impression. In order to start a meaningful discussion, we must establish credibility without bragging or talking about ourselves. How do we do that? If the focus is on getting a meeting with management, there are words to use that position us more as peers than sales people. In his book, *Value Forward Selling*, Paul Dimodica, has a great list of peer-sounding words to be used when setting a meeting.

Vendor Sounding Words	Peer Sounding Words
Sales	Chat or Coffee
Appointment	Meeting
Deal	Firm
Company	Engage
Discuss	Strategic Focus
Contract	Scorecard
Demo	Tactical Use
Presentation	Productivity Improvement
Proposal	Performance Improvement
Invoice	Executive Briefing
Purchase Order	Business Value
Pilot or Test Order	Return on Investment
Order	Strategic Value
Technology	Value Driven
Software	

DiModica

Cold Calling

Based upon my cold calling story at the beginning of the book, one might be surprised to see the topic of cold calling in this chapter. Cold calling can be the bane of a seller's existence! It scared me to death in the beginning of my career, and sometimes it still does. You do not have to be proficient at cold calling in order to be successful in sales as long as you build a highly connected network and focus on relationships.

So why include this section? Sometimes we just have to make a call to someone we do not know. The reality is, cold calling can work, and we all need to practice techniques even when we are making friendly calls or informational calls. If you can become comfortable calling strangers and practicing networking scripts, it will get easier over time to deal with rejection. Remember, there will be opportunities in a career to teach and mentor others and unless you can do it, it is difficult to teach. Cold calling is no different. As an up and coming leader, I knew I would have to master the art of cold calling, even though I believed there were more effective ways to get meetings. Here are some guidelines:

- Write down several scenarios of your networking pitch and know the objective of your call. What do you want out of this call?

- Structure the time and block out everything else. This is calling time and the more distractions you eliminate, the better. If you

are calling executives remember they start early and work late so call them before their assistant gets there or after they leave.

- Have all the names, addresses, and phone numbers in front of you either in a list in an automated sales system or on a piece of paper. If you get in a groove, you want to keep the momentum going.

- Set up your time in one-hour increments and keep track of dials, messages, answers, and successful calls per hour. You cannot manage what you cannot measure.

- Give yourself little rewards throughout the day like a cup of coffee, a cold drink, or a walk around the office or lunch.

- When you get a meeting set, call someone and celebrate.

Remember, it is not about you. If you are honest and cordial and do not use tricks, people will appreciate that. I also always ask, "is this is a convenient time to talk?" or if there is another time that would be better. If they say that they have a minute or two, move quickly to tell them why you are calling and what you want. If they say they are not the right person, ask if they could give you the name and extension of the right person. If they want to reschedule, have two times ready. "Mr. Jones, would you like to talk tomorrow at 3 p.m. or Wednesday at 2 p.m. CST?" I have also heard of networkers who send an email to the person and specify the time and date that they will be calling. Once you realize that

rejection is not personal, then it just becomes another competition where you are challenging yourself to improve. Keep in mind that instant access to information has transferred power in the sales cycle from sellers to buyers. Buyers are often further down the sales cycle than you realize and when you show up they have looked at your website, your LinkedIn profile and may have sought a reference. This makes it even more critical to be prepared.

Chapter 15 - Proposing and Winning

The First Meeting – It's About the Customer

Plan for the first meeting to last about twenty minutes. That way, the executives see that you appreciate the most valuable thing they have, their time. If the executive only has 20 minutes, the conversation should focus on something unique that preparation has uncovered about the company, and how your offerings will deliver value. The goal is scheduling a follow-up meeting. Experience has taught me that the purpose of a meeting is to get another meeting. It is like introducing an idea to the prospect and having them say "tell me more." Booking the second meeting infers that the preparation before the first meeting has resonated with the prospect. I know that a meeting is going well if the executive lets the meeting continue beyond the specified 20 minutes. The goal in the first meeting is to establish credibility, prove capabilities, and schedule a follow-up meeting. Being authentic and genuine is critical to success. Selling hard is a turn off for most executives.

Many of us were taught that there are generally three ways to begin a discussion. First, talk about your company in an outlined page-by-page company overview; second, talk about your services; or third, ask open-ended questions to begin the conversation. None of these approaches give the prospect the feeling of being in control. The worst

presenters start flipping through a long presentation that eats up the time and does not focus on the prospect. Stop. Do not take a deck. Do not talk about yourself. Do not just start asking questions! Instead, take heed from Kevin Daly in *Socratic Selling*. In the Socratic method, Daly discusses three choices:

1. **Be Prepared to Speak** - "I'm prepared to talk about

   _____ "

2. **Invite the Customer to Speak** – "I'm prepared to talk about

   _____, which we discussed on the phone. If you could give me your perspective on that . . . "

3. **Offer an Immediate Benefit** – "I'm prepared to talk about

   _____, which we discussed on the phone. If you could give me your perspective on that, we can focus the meeting on what interests you."

The immediate benefit strategy gives control to the prospect and puts the seller in a position to give the prospect something of value in the first ten minutes of the meeting. Now contrast this technique with what most other sales people do in a first meeting. They start talking about themselves, their company, and their product rather than the client. Because most prospects do not know all that a company has to offer, let them start with their own requests and allow them to control the process while they become more educated.

Closing the Meeting

If the initial meeting goes well, you will move to schedule a follow-up meeting with a bigger group, or you will begin to lay the ground work for the sales process. Because credibility has been established, you can set expectations about the best process to get to a solution. These are the steps that allow you to create a winning solution, penetrate the company, and position your firm to win. Establishing the right sales process is the first negotiation with a client. Using a process to help the prospect get to the best solution is an important tool. The posture used in setting up the right process will set the tone for future negotiations. Conducting small negotiations along the way will improve your chances of success. If you are not establishing a process or redirecting a client's request, it is very hard to win. The exchange would sound something like this:

"Joe, we enjoyed getting to know you today and believe we have the capabilities that will assist you in improving

_____. Let me take a moment to describe the process that we go through, which gets us both to the best outcome. It also gives both parties the opportunity to exit the process if we discover there is not a fit. We understand that we might not be the best fit for your firm or we might get to the point where we realize that our approach is not the best way to

address your challenge. This way, we can work together for a common outcome. Is that fair?"

Most reasonable people will agree that the process you outline is fair. If not, move on and find a different prospect. The goal is to win, not just be engaged in activity. If you cannot sell the way you want, it is unlikely you will win.

"Here are some of the activities that our firm outlines to ensure we achieve the right benefits for your firm and ours. Each step includes a Go/No Go decision for each of us so either one of us can opt out at any time."

What you are describing to the prospect is a sales process that will leave you in the best light and allow you to prove your value. The first step is discovery. Because consulting is about solving problems, consultants believe that gathering requirements is the sole reason to do discovery. "We scope the project and prepare a proposal, right?" Yes and no. It is true that you need the details of a problem in order to create a proposal; however, this is also the one time that a company will give a consulting firm broad access to a wide range of employees. As you navigate the organization gathering requirements, learn the organization and create a power map as discussed in Chapter 11. Taking the time now will enable you to set up a winning sales strategy by knowing the players in the game. If all you have at the end of discovery is a list of requirements, it is

likely that you will have missed something critical that would help you win.

The following excerpt from *Hope is Not a Strategy* states the objective perfectly:

Understanding the client's need is the heart of consultative selling. It changes the initial direction of information flow to problems in search of solutions, instead of the other way around. What problem is the customer trying to solve? Although we use the term "pain," this could also be an opportunity. The art of consultative selling is to get the customer talking in a one-on-one environment, sharing who they are and what they want. Consultative salespeople learn early that the way to get the client talking is to use questions that begin with "who, what, why, when, or where."

This is a critical part of the sale because we begin listening and "out caring" the competition, thus building the bonds of rapport that will eventually lead to trust. Even if we know what the pains are, it is not enough. The client needs to confess them. Confession is the beginning behavior modification, and, for a consultant, starts a sharing process that begins to build the bonds of trust. Then, when we do present, we can focus on the needs that have been expressed, in the client's terminology, with friends in the audience, without being set up by the competition.

It is critical that your emotional intelligence gathering mechanism is as tuned in as your intellectual capacity. If not, it is easy to overlook an emotional or political landmine. Early in my career, I walked through a prospect's office and saw a sales deck (presentation) from a competing consultancy on the desk of one of the executives. By paying attention and gathering organizational information, you will improve the odds of winning. It is important to spend as much time developing a power map as gathering detailed requirements. Discovery is about learning, listening, and preparing your company to win.

As you begin the discovery process, there are several insights to define as you sort out requirements, pain, and a potential solution. It is best to break down the walls and learn about the organization at the beginning of the process. You can ask for access during this period because you have something the client wants, a proposal. Once the proposal is delivered many of those doors close and the opportunity to gain insight is lost. When credibility is established and pain is identified, it is critical to move quickly and define a winning strategy. There are several questions to ask when developing a winning strategy:

- Is there competition?
    - Are we behind?
    - Is the IT department our real competition?
    - Is the deal competitive?
- What is the organizational culture?
    - Are they open or closed?
    - Is it autocratic or consensus?

- o Who is the cultural fit from your firm?
- Do you know the organizational structure?
  - o Who has the official power? (this is the org chart)
  - o Who has the informal power? (this is gleaned through interviews)
- What is the decision-making process?
  - o Individual?
  - o Committee?
  - o Relationship?
  - o Last best argument?
- How are decisions made?
  - o Pet project?
  - o Revenue enhancement?
  - o Expense reduction?
- Do you have an internal coach?
  - o Sponsor?
  - o Power?
  - o Dissenter?
  - o Pragmatist?

The discovery process involves canvassing the organization, talking to as many individuals as possible, not just one or two. Do not get stuck with one person at the beginning of a cycle, or you will never be able to maneuver later, when you really want and need the information.

Next, set up an executive briefing based upon what your firm has discovered. The purpose of the executive briefing is to gain credibility and make sure that no lower level manager can hijack your process or findings. On many occasions, I have had private one-on-one discussions with senior executives where I shared something that they did not know about their organization. Executives appreciate the insight. After the briefing, move towards a confirmation stage where a pre-

proposal is delivered rather than a statement of work. Most consultancies conduct discovery and then work diligently on building a word document that is known as a statement of work (SOW). By skipping the pre-proposal step, the seller increases the risk of missing something and losing the opportunity to build the most effective power map. What if your proposal is slightly off from what the company really wants? Also, executives will flip through a short deck before they will read a 3-page SOW. Delivering an SOW is like sending a signal to the executive to send you to their procurement or legal organization.

I learned this the hard way by working hard on a proposal and emailing it to my contact. That was the last I heard from them. I reached out via phone and email but never made contact. Eventually, I was informed that we lost. When I asked the prospect why, the answer was that our solution was off base. We missed something and never got a second chance. During a different sales process, we went through discovery and were going to start working on the proposal. In an internal planning session, our team disagreed about what our approach should be and what the real problem was that they wanted us to solve. I suggested that we call the senior executive with whom we had established rapport and set a meeting where we could ask some additional questions. I was honest about our emphatic disagreement internally and he found the fact that we actively disagreed amongst

ourselves endearing. Rather than delivering a draft SOW, we built a deck that had findings, diagrams, bullets, and questions. That led to an interactive white-board session where the customer took out a pen and drew lines and made notes on our hard copy presentation. While preparing the final document, I looked at the deck and discovered the client had told us exactly what he wanted and how much he was willing to pay. With that story, the pre-proposal was born, and I rarely skip that step today. In fact, when I do not do a pre-proposal it is because the customer is in a hurry or I am confident in my relationship with the client. Skipping the pre-proposal usually ends poorly. What I have learned over time is that by using this technique, a proposal went from being my idea to becoming the client's solution. By the time a final proposal is delivered, there is no new information and the probability of winning is high.

This technique confirms your firm's understanding, approach, scope, and cost. It allows the team to have an interactive and iterative session(s) with the buyer where the buyer transitions from the proposal being *our proposal to their proposal*. This transition is important to the overall sales process because it allows the buyer to internalize the solution. Once this transition happens, the hook is set, and the buyer has emotional ownership. They rarely change their minds.

If a seller skips this step and delivers an SOW, there are a couple of things that can happen. First, the seller misses what the client really wants. Sellers miss things all the time. Sometimes it is your team's fault because you are not actively listening for what the buyer wants to buy and other times it is because the buyer may not be sure of what they really want. Second, if you have not talked about price or budget, you are likely to price yourself out of the deal before they understand the value you are creating. With the pre-proposal, you work through issues with a buyer by "sharing some ideas" or "validating that we are going in the right direction." It is an extra step, but well worth it.

The best tool for the pre-proposal is a short, well-crafted deck but can also be in a summary document or well-crafted email. In larger deals where you are meeting face-to-face, the deck is the best strategy. For the small or narrowly defined deal, keep it simple and summarize in an email. The deck is non-threatening and one can stamp "draft" all over the document with terms like "illustrative." The buyer does not realize that at this point we are beginning the negotiation process. The seller is also leaving them with a tool that they can use for internal selling. You can count on that deck traveling around to constituents in the organization, many of whom you have not met. Many people will not read a proposal, but they will speed read a short deck. The buyer leverages

the deck while gaining support for their initiative and they are using the language your firm created in the pre-proposal.

The purpose of the deck is to tell a story while getting the prospect to visualize the solution and fees. The pre-proposal is everything one needs to engage the client in a meaningful discussion while still giving your firm the opportunity to make corrections to the final written proposal. As the seller guides the prospect through the process, the prospect's ownership increases. The transition of ownership is not only important to make sure you are on the right track with the problem you want to solve, but the process also helps to create alignment with the executive.

The Deck

Table of Contents

Our Understanding, 1 page – Simple, straightforward, to the point

Our Solution, 1-2 pages -- Length depends on complexity and scope

Our Approach, 1 page-- Details depend on how much detail the client needs

Fees and License, 1 page, Depends on the complexity of the solution

If the seller orchestrates the pre-proposal correctly, the final proposal is accepted because there won't be any new information for the buyer to process. You can use the following words: "By the time we give you a proposal, there will be no new information." A skilled seller will

have set up a process where the buyer will come to the desired conclusion and hopefully, will have modified enough of the details so they internalize the final version of the proposal as theirs. Remember, people support what they help to create.

Proposal

The proposal is the written word of what was in the pre-proposal following the same general outline. Often, the seller can use the graphics that were used in the pre-proposal and leverage them in the proposal. Choose your approach based upon the size of the company, value of the deal, and the complexity of the solution.

Controlling the Process

Notice that the heading says to control the process and not the buyer. A sales cycle is about facilitating an outcome without forcing the buyer to move unless moving is their idea. Of course, part of the art of persuasion is delivering evidence to the buyer and allowing them to decide in your favor. There is no mystery if you use a process. It is an art for sure! By being a facilitator and not a seller, you will gain an advantage. Let the buyer buy, in their time. Often external pressures affect sellers at this point. Either because of pressure that the business is putting on them (economic challenges), or an office is putting on them (not making enough contribution). This is the time to be patient. Never close or push the buyer when they are not ready. The art of the deal is moving the

buyer along in the process, leaving them in control. I worked a large deal at a regional telecom when I was at Ariba but working it through a reseller of our B2B platform. We had started the final negotiation in the beginning of Q4 of that year, and the leaves were turning. The process lengthened because our proposal had to go through legal but to get the offer we were proposing, the buyer needed to sign the contract by year end. I remember how frustrated my channel partner and I were when the process slowed to a crawl, but we never took it out on the client. We knew that time killed deals and the longer it went, the more likely it would be to go away, but we just kept nudging it along. We had good executive level contacts but needed to get through legal. We were in daily, multi-hour negotiations on the language, and paragraph by paragraph we were starting to make it through. Late one Friday afternoon as we were in contract negotiations with the buyer, I heard their chief legal counsel say, "Oh no!"

I knew he had been working at home during an ice storm and the "oh no" was him telling us that the power had just gone out. The next couple of days fell over the Christmas holiday, so I thought the deal was over. On December 30th, we finished negotiations and looked for the CFO to sign the proposal, but he had headed home for the holiday and nobody told us. It did not take my channel partner much time to get on a plane with the contract, fly to Chicago, drive to the CFOs home in the

snow (you cannot make this stuff up) and get the contract signed. He even got a picture of the CFO in his running attire at the kitchen table, but we got the deal done because we were patient, and willing to go the extra mile.

NEVER CLOSE UNTIL A DEAL IS READY TO BE CLOSED!

You will know. A prospect will tell you. If you push a bad position, there will be unintended consequences. It is a fact! The point is to make sure that you guide the process and do not try to control the buyer. Buyers are empowered by believing they are in control of the process. If you have created the right vision of a solution, you have an internal coach at the buyer's company, and you have outlined the sales process, the buyer will track right along with what you have outlined. The buyer will feel ownership and control of the process.

There is no greater feeling as a seller than when you win a deal and the buyer tells you why they selected you. In between the lines one will hear many of the points made during the process. It is a thing of beauty to execute a winning plan and be rewarded for it. In the end, if one is selling something of value, at a fair price, then it is about winning. There is no prize for second place.

Conclusion

There is no short cut for a complex deal. I can tell many anecdotes that occurred in my career where I thought because of a relationship, lack of a competitor, or the superiority of my solution - that I could skip a step.

I remember when I realized this process really worked as I was training a young seller on a sizeable transaction. Because I was also coaching other members of my team on other opportunities, I would meet regularly with my junior person and we would script out every conversation and meeting. We followed the steps to the tee and won the deal. The tragedy of it was he thought he was responsible for winning the deal and immediately went to the regional sales manager to say he was ready for a full quota and territory. He was not and ultimately failed. It is important to realize that connecting and selling is both art and science. A seller needs to develop discipline around creating meaningful activities, so they become second nature. As you experience success, posture will develop and lead you to walk away from a transaction if you can't implement a process that is proven to yield success.

Whenever I teach a workshop, I try to emphasize how important it is to stay on message and on target until one experiences the outcomes outlined in these pages. The process is the shortcut.

Chapter 16 - Negotiation and Closing

We've all been in situations where we did the right thing at the wrong time and lost a deal. Negotiation and closing are areas fraught with disaster because winning is tough enough, but closing can be volatile.

The first challenge that one grapples with is whether or not the proposal you submitted won the deal before the client tells you officially. Most of the content of this book surrounds addressing how to connect externally and to use a variety of tools to create business opportunities for your firm. Entering the negotiation phase and knowing where your firm is across the spectrum of winning, provides the posture necessary for negotiation. Sometimes you will find yourself at the end of a sales cycle and discover you have lost. If this is the case, resist the temptation to panic. Instead stop and think about how you can change the deal or raise fear, uncertainty, or doubt (FUD) about the competition. At this point, winning is not likely but understanding where your process failed is important.

In all cases, stay on the high road because you want your company to be known as the one with high integrity. You should be interested in a relationship for the next 100 years and not just the next 100 days. Even in losing, the goal is to consider how to be more effective at developing long-term relationships, which will lead to success. Recall

my experience when my last company was just two people and the lead was a result of losing an earlier opportunity.

After understanding where the deal is in the process, prepare for negotiations. As you prepare, remember that a buyer's concerns shift throughout the sales or visioning process. Whether dealing with a new buyer, or pitching a new idea to an existing client, the buyer's concerns change from *need and a vision* of the solution to *risk and cost.*

The words your prospect used at the beginning of the process become less important as the deal nears a decision point. Most prospects are not even aware that they go through this transition. Do not get confused between the "negotiation game" (to be addressed later in this chapter) with valid concerns that could derail the project should your answer be inadequate.

What Can You Negotiate?

Knowing what can and cannot be negotiated is critical to finalizing a deal. There is a give and take between buyer and seller that is as much art as science. Back up your instincts with a good framework and process.

Shifting Buyer Concerns

Two good books on the topic of shifting buyer concerns are *Hope is Not a Strategy* by Rick Page and *Solution Selling* by Michael Bosworth. While they differ slightly in the steps they use, they are conceptually the

same. For the purposes of this discussion, I will use Bosworth's model and pepper it with ideas from Page.

Buyers generally have four different concerns as they think about purchasing solutions:

- Do I have a **NEED**?

- Do I have a **SOLUTION** to my need?

- What will be the **COST**?

- What is the **RISK** of buying, or not buying?

The four questions listed above are not product related, commodity related, services related, or anything but human behavior related. The buyer needs to evaluate whether your firm created the right vision of a solution, then they must consider how they will pay for that solution. Finally, they will explore the risks that might derail the project, put their reputation in a bad light, or potentially get them fired. These are the considerations that buyers are evaluating throughout the process.

Within those four questions of need, solution, price, and risk, buyers go through three basic phases of considerations as they think about finalizing an engagement.

- **Phase I** – Need Definition

- **Phase II** – Evaluation of Alternatives

- **Phase III** – Taking Action within Risk Considerations

Understanding where the prospective company is throughout the sales cycle will keep you selling the right aspect of the deal at the right time. Using the following graphic, it is easy to understand why a seller needs to qualify both the solution and the investment a prospect will need to make early in a sale process.

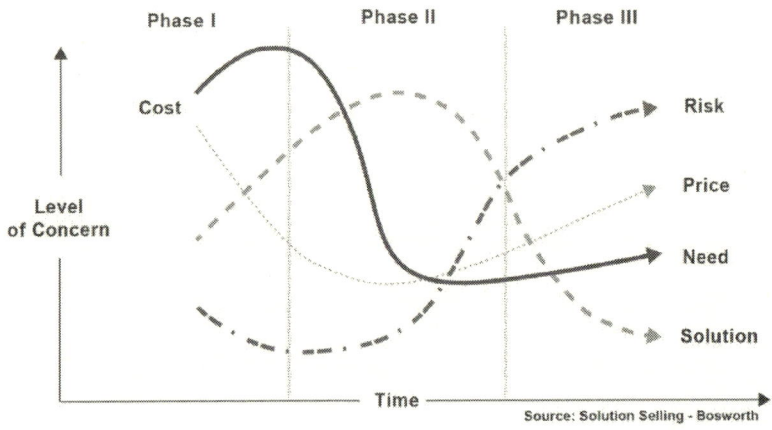

Source: Solution Selling - Bosworth

Take some time and study this chart. I can tell you many stories of selling individuals who were still pitching features and functions at the end of the sales cycle when the buyer was considering the risk associated with the project. I fell into this trap early in my career at Lawson. I was selling to a large private company that managed golf courses. Near the end of the sales cycle, I was still talking about our solution, and why we were uniquely qualified to meet their needs, whereas my competition was talking about the risk of going with a software that didn't have a global solution implemented in multiple

languages and currencies. At the end of the decision process, the CFO was worried about their international operations because they represented the growth through future acquisitions. I was selling features and functions, and my competition was selling safety and security at the right time in the cycle. He won!

Rick Page nails this dichotomy on the head when he says:

"The bad news is that at this point the client is asking you all sorts of nasty, snarling legal questions. The good news is that the client is asking you these nasty, snarling legal questions. If after your capabilities presentation they are not asking you risk questions, they are not thinking about doing business with you."

As you consider the progression through these phases, there are certain questions a seller must know to determine where the buyer is in the process.

Phase I – Need Definition

- ***Buyer is asking "need" questions…***
    - Do I need to change?
    - What are the reasons for my problems?
    - Who does it impact?
    - How much will it cost?
    - Have you provided a vision of the solution?

Phase II – Evaluation of Alternatives

- ***Buyer evaluates alternatives*** with questions…

    - Is there really a solution?

    - Which alternative best meets my needs?

    - Can I afford it?

    - Who do I want to work with?

    - Can I do it myself without external help?

    - Is doing nothing an option?

Phase III – Taking action within risk considerations

- ***Having made a mental selection***, the buyer advances to risk-reward questions…

    - Should I do it?

    - What if I don't? What are the consequences?

    - Is it the right price? Am I getting the best deal/value?

    - What is the ROI? When will I get the pay back?

    - Is my organization ready? (change management)

    - Can the vendor deliver on what he has promised?

While every sales cycle is different, a seller can anticipate what the buyer's thinking is and focus on selling the next phase of the sale. Do not

get too far ahead of the process and mistakenly believe the process is finished.

It is also possible that if one is meeting with several executives from a company, they may be in different phases at the same time. As a seller, you may need to reinforce your capabilities for one person in the audience while mitigating the emotional risk for the other executives. Sensing these dynamics in real time is approaching mastery and will make you a good teacher. At this point in the cycle, reflect upon the company power map and relationships established throughout the sales cycle. Try to prove to your team whether your proposal is winning or not. This is the reason I try to avoid going alone to big meetings at the end of a sales cycle. Often, while you are cycling on solution or vision creation, your colleague is sensing another dynamic that may be at work. This is why team selling is important. Part of your sales strategy should be to learn as much as possible, so you understand the human dynamic. Use the members of your team to back channel the prospect and gather information that could bolster your position.

Staying aligned with the client is a critical skill.

Phase I – Qualify Needs and the Buying Process

- Our mission is to **create a vision** for the buyer or **re-engineer an existing vision**.

- Qualify how the buyer/organization will buy.

- Align your sales process to the buyer's buying process.

Phase II – Prove and Help Buyer Justify Cost

- Our mission is to **prove** and help the buyer **justify the cost**.

- Proof can be provided with case studies, testimonials, benchmarks, demonstrations, presentations, etc.

- We must give proof, even if we have influenced the vision.

- We must re-engineer existing competitive visions, if we intend to compete. If we align our services with an existing vision created by a competitor, we will end up as column fodder (column fodder refers to your company being in column B or C but not in column A)

- Cost or **value justification is the extra mile** that many competitors skip. ROI is king!

Phase III – Close the Sale

- If the buyer shows you his fear of risk, the deal is yours to lose.
- The buyer **ONLY** gets into Phase III when the solution fits and the costs are justified.
- **Buyers will need comfort and reassurance**, even if the risks are minimal.

What else can go wrong? One of the reasons that Page and Bosworth disagree on what the most crucial factor is at the end of a sales cycle is because risk and price/cost are often equal in importance and the buyer seems to slip very quickly between the two. Once the buyer checks the box on the solution and you have mitigated the risk, things can still go wrong.

Somebody is always tasked with getting the best deal. They assume that your company has not given them the best deal, and they will want to play the negotiation game. You'll hear things such as, "Several firms can meet our needs, but your price is higher." Suddenly the client can't tell the difference between your solution and the competition's. In larger companies, the procurement organization gets involved and not only do they not understand the differences in your solution, they don't care. All those weeks or months of work seem to

evaporate. Page calls this "convenient amnesia" but points out that this language means you are in the game.

Price negotiations are a difficult and emotional process for both the seller and the buyer. Each party must overcome specific emotional hurdles before consummating a contract. The process requires planning and preparation to anticipate what the client needs, develop a set of alternatives, and practice or think through those conversations. You need to know the buyer and think about how they buy. And you must have the intestinal fortitude to walk away if a fair deal cannot be reached.

Lessons

Below are some advisory nuggets that a seller should internalize while in the negotiation phase:

Lesson 1: Protect Your Price

- If you must concede, concede on something other than on price.
- Ramifications can extend to other buyers in a similar industry or marketplace, so you must acknowledge the possibility that your buyers may communicate with each other.

Lesson 2: Don't Give Without Getting

- Memorize this important negotiation phrase: "The only way I could do something for you is if you could do something for me in return." This puts the buyer in the position to inquire, "Like what?"

- Retain seller's position in the driver's seat. In other words, allow the buyer to be in charge, but do not roll over on everything without getting something in return.

- Giving without getting during the negotiation can become a death spiral with the buyer leading you deeper by encouraging you that indeed you are "getting closer, just one last thing..."

Lesson 3: The Seller Has to Draw the Line First

- Alternatives and Go/No Go points must be developed and reviewed internally prior to key meetings. This requires planning and preparation.

- Taking a stand on key points in the process articulates to the buyer that as a seller, you have limits and will not roll over for every request.

- As noted above, by not giving without getting, the seller ensures the process maintains an important sequence allowing the seller to retain the power position.

Conclusion

Negotiation is where every seller wants to be because it means you won the deal. It can be characterized as the beginning of the second half of a contest, but it starts early in the sales process as you establish credibility and posture. I tell people often that they have to say "no" three times in a sales process to win. If you wait until the negotiation stage, it's too late.

Sophisticated buyers understand the process, and they know more about you than you think. Do not assume anything during this phase of the pursuit and hold the cards close to your vest. With some planning and a little faith you will get the outcome you want.

Chapter 17 – Managing Business from a Dashboard

Remember the acronym KISS – Keep It Simple Stupid! Managing a sales team is as much about art as science. The knee-jerk response of most senior executives is to implement a Customer Relationship Management (CRM) system so that every interaction with a prospect and/or client can be tracked and measured. The challenge is that these systems are takers from sales people and not helpers. Let me explain. Individuals who sell for a living tend to be less structured and organized and yet, companies want them to enter all of these interactions in a system so that management can review their progress. On the other hand, our Touchpoints software is designed to help the individual seller. When management pushes employees for strict compliance, they tend to get malicious compliance – meaning, the employee does what you say but the data is unreliable. Another type of pipeline manager is the technician who is very conservative and so when looking at a pipeline, it is hard to see what is going to close because the individual is overly conservative. They are not willing to put an estimate out there and have it be wrong. This is usually because their personality is precise and they don't want to disappoint others. The data is accurate, but the projection of revenue does not match with the sales and margin needs of the business.

I have managed both the overly aggressive forecaster and the ultra-conservative forecaster and have come to the conclusion that less is more. The keep-it-simple-stupid method is the best approach for helping a company manage its pipeline. The reason for having a sales process is so that we can determine if our pipeline is adequate to meet the sales and margin goals of the business. Every company is different, but each must define a clear set of activities to be completed in a stage of a sales cycle and that are associated with a probability of winning. Yes, all of those features of a richer customer relationship management system (CRM) would be cool, but if a company can't implement it to get accurate information, is it worth the effort? I've observed that, from time to time, it was not unusual for something to go from lead to closed without going through each step of the process. This happens a lot in consulting firms but it makes it difficult to balance the number of consultants who are not working and the sales needed to keep them busy. When managing a pipeline, one needs to strike a balance between process and the personalities of those involved.

Every sales process is different but there are some common steps in putting it all together. The goal is to keep it simple, and to communicate the actions that are necessary at each phase of the cycle. You will want to make these steps applicable to your business and the solutions you are selling. Once completed, the company will have a

common tribal language so that everyone in the company is doing the

same activities in the same stage of a sales cycle. The following

Touchpoints template is a good start.

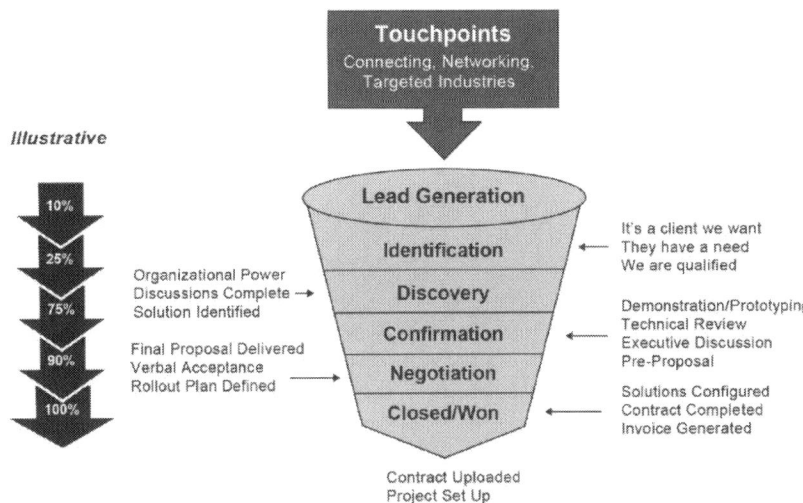

In the chart above, the sales process is illustrated by identifying a few

statements or activities used to remind the seller where they are in the

sales cycle. The tribal language referenced in the previous paragraph is

very important, especially as the business grows. If a company does not

have everyone in the company calling the sales steps the same thing,

then it is difficult to forecast revenue. It is ineffective if each seller brings

their own version of the truth to weekly sales meetings because it inhibits

accurate forecasting.

Put the Pipeline in Your Terms

The other area I would insist on from a pipeline management perspective is that you put the numbers in your terms. If you are a services company and trade hours for dollars, then every opportunity should be for a number of full-time equivalents (FTEs) at a blended rate per hour for a number of hours per month.

Example:

You think you can sell a six-week technology assessment for 2.5 people.

2.5 x $175 x 43 x 6 = $112,875

FTE x Rate x Hours Per Week x Weeks = Total Engagement

In the pipeline, one might put $75,250 in the month you start the engagement and $37,625 in the following month. Companies typically pay their employees twice per month so you can always compare your current backlog (work in progress) with your pipeline to see if you will cover your overhead. By following this methodology, you enforce a rigor on your team to determine what they really think the opportunity value is to the organization. If the company quantifies pipeline in the same terms as it does backlog, then the company is comparing apples with apples. Backlog is defined as work sold, not yet delivered and it is calculated in terms of the number of people billing at a specified rate into the future by month. Pipeline opportunities need to be presented in a similar manner.

Often consultants have a deal identified for a company but don't know what to put into the deal in terms of dollars. My perspective is that if the opportunity is a client we want, the company has a need and your company is qualified to do the work, then a dollar amount guestimate can be inserted. Once quantified as a client you want and work you can do, the opportunity enters the top of the funnel as an identified opportunity. The next step is to enforce how you track the probability of winning. I like to discount opportunities based upon sales stage because the stage is tied to a set of activities.

Identification (10% probability of success)

The first step of the process is to identify the market you are targeting. The narrower the focus, the better. Consider revenue and industry when defining your target market. For example, you might choose to sell to a $100 million division of a billion-dollar company that is engaged in selling engineering services. These are organizations that you would like to do business with because they meet your criteria as a client and fit your target profile. These are not companies who just have needs. As we have discussed throughout the book, focus, focus, focus.

Discovery (25% probability of success)

Discovery starts with a conversation and ends with an understanding of what products or services result in a solution. In the middle, we need access to the power players to figure out who makes the decisions.

Understanding the organizational structure, culture, and political landscape of the company is paramount to a successful sales process. The seller must understand who is sponsoring the project and how decisions are made. The seller is also trying to develop a coach. The sponsor and coach are rarely the same person at larger accounts and are usually the same person at smaller companies. Remember, the discovery process is as much about learning the political and power structure at the company as it is determining the problem that requires a solution.

Confirmation (75% probability of success)

Confirmation requires a lot of activity and you can dial in the probability from 60% to 75%. If sellers can consistently accomplish all of the key activities defined, the probability of success increases. Activities include a demonstration of the platform and various solutions followed by a technical discussion, or an architecture or business process discussion. This could be something new or a scoped proof of concept in a PowerPoint presentation that highlights what you have learned about the account. Finally, the seller sends a pre-proposal and a sample contract. When this stage is complete, the seller should have a good idea on the chances of winning. If the seller does not know, then the deal is probably still in the discovery stage or not all the way through confirmation.

Negotiation (90% probability of success)

During negotiation, deliver a final proposal along with terms and conditions with the solutions attached. Look for a verbal approval followed by a plan to get the solution into production in an incremental way or a project started.

Closed/Won (100% probability of success)

At this point, the contract is signed, implementation planning has begun, and a kick off meeting is scheduled.

As mentioned earlier, pipeline management is as much art as science. The science I describe above has some artistic flair and is subject to interpretation. The percentages we assign to each phase, above, are called the Weighted Average Pipeline (WAP).

These are conservative percentages multiplied by the total value of the pipeline at each stage. By weighting the entire pipeline, a company can have a single number to evaluate on a monthly basis that helps to determine if the collection of deals, weighted as defined, is large enough to sustain the enterprise or division. It also tells the company where the cashflow cliff is months out from the current date.

This strategy is not without criticism. The critics say that a company doesn't win a percent of a deal but rather it *wins* or it *loses*. The WAP is still an effective tool as it allows conservative sellers to put a deal

in identification at a decent value and only have a small percentage drop to the bottom line. The purpose of the WAP is to understand if the company has a critical mass of opportunities to meet the cash needs of the business. In the dashboard below, the company knows exactly what the backlog is when compared to a discounted pipeline and where the estimated cliff is for the business. The cliff is defined as the moment when backlog is insufficient to cover the cash burn of the business and the numbers turn red.

If management continues to review deals and requires strict enforcement of activities in a stage, the result is a discounted pipeline by month added to a backlog (work sold not yet worked) by month. In this way, it is clear what the cash needs of the business are looking into the future.

Sales Operation Dashboard

Fiscal Year Pipeline	Fiscal Year Backlog	Fiscal Year Estimated Revenue	Forecasted Sales
$ 25,758,000	$ 23,728,000	$ 23,200,000	$ 25,000,000

Weighted Average Pipeline	Fiscal Year Booked	Fiscal Year Estimated Sales	Weighted Pipeline Shortfall
$ 20,758,000	$ 23,758,000	$ 20,728,000	$ 23,000,000

	20 Jan	20 Feb	20 Mar	20 Apr	20 May	20 Jun
Pipeline						
Weighted Pipeline						
Revenue						
Burn						
Sales To Burn						
Forecast						
Sales To Forecast						

The dashboard illustrated above can be implemented in a number of pipeline management tools including SalesForce. Because it is designed for services companies who sell services for a living, it creates the same context for pipeline as it does backlog. The system tracks opportunities through a pipeline and compares the backlog with the burn rate of the business. This methodology is lightweight for a reason. The implementation of a heavy customer/ relationship management system is difficult at best for many reasons. These systems are complex, require organizational change, and are integrated to legacy systems of record.

The key is to create a dashboard that you can use to manage the business on a day to day basis, while creating a language that both aggressive and conservative leaders are comfortable with. When you consistently know where you are success comes more easily.

Creating Your Plan

It has been said that the difference between success and failure is the 12 inches between one's head and heart. As with most things in life, just a little more knowledge is not the answer to success. Ralph Waldo Emerson said, "Nothing great was ever achieved without enthusiasm." While a pipeline is important to the health of any services organization, the behavior of the individual rolls up into the performance of the enterprise. The goal of this book has been to provide the skills necessary to be a successful business developer for the firm. As individuals, we are responsible for moving the effort from the head to the heart. Implementing these techniques is up to you.

As you work toward developing a plan for your company, determine which tools presented in this book are helpful to you and which ones are not. For instance, take the anecdote or stories which you now know are a critical part of selling techniques. You have to make a story your own, told with your personality and your capabilities.

Goal Setting

Lewis Carroll, the famous English novelist and mathematician, is best known for his written work *Alice's Adventures in Wonderland*. One of the great quotes of a dialogue exchange from that book is:

> *"But I don't want to go among mad people," said Alice. "Oh, you can't help that," said the cat. "We're all mad here."*

It is true that we all have to be a little mad to be in this chosen profession. The work is difficult, the hours are long, and the clients are demanding, but the rewards and sense of accomplishment are wonderful. Many may not know that Lewis Carroll is also known to have said, "If you don't know where you are going, any road will get you there." We've heard derivatives of this phrase throughout our lives. By now we all know that we have to set goals, but there is a defense mechanism that we all have, a little voice inside our heads that says, "If I don't set a goal, then I can't fail." Do not kid yourself. We fail because we do not set our own goals.

Perhaps you have heard the phrase, "Goals are in concrete, plans are in sand." In other words, we work and live in a fast-paced environment and while circumstances may affect our plans to reach our goals, they should never affect the goals themselves. We should all be setting attainable goals that we can measure in realistic time frames.

One of the roles of a coach is to push those being coached farther than they can push themselves, and my goal with this book is no different. In giving you the skills, you must also accept the responsibility that goes along with the skills. You must use those tools, measure the results, and strive to improve. You cannot accomplish these things without setting a goal and then working a plan.

Tell somebody!

If a tree falls in the forest and nobody is there, does it make any sound? If I am gathering wood for a fire and stumble upon your tree in the woods, I really do not care if it made noise. I have the wood!

The most important thing you can do when setting goals, is to tell someone else. Then, set up a system or pattern for communicating to the person to whom you are accountable. Once an opportunity is found and moved through a pipeline, it is easy to track deals sold or revenue generated. However, if you are actively working and growing an account or penetrating a target account, you better have a system for communicating results to constituents and bosses. If there is no communication, then the lack of positive outcomes will affect you negatively. Most organizations will look at your performance as a reflection of your success. Set realistic goals, work towards completing them successfully, and be accountable for them.

Chapter 18 - Bringing it all Together

Well, that's it! Even after reading the material you need to put things to work to see what works. Focus on making a working plan. Remember, you need to be in the business of client enablement – giving tools to customers to enable their businesses to grow, lower costs, and reduce risk. Establishing consistent habits around networking and selling is the most valuable thing a knowledge worker can do. There are companies out there who need the solutions that you are qualified to deliver. Building a network and connecting with people in a meaningful way will accomplish this goal. Many of you are getting exposure to this information for the first time, so be patient with yourself. Remember, selling is a process by which we solve a problem for an individual or company. Take your time, ask good questions, and use the methods you have learned here.

Hopefully you have seen how connecting for life will create opportunities for you to give to others around you. For me, I was initially looking for a short cut to generate revenue as an individual. Later in my career, I looked at *Connect for Life* as a methodology that could be taught across a wide range of knowledge workers to help them succeed. This idea is not unique or new since companies formed as partnerships have been doing this for years. The challenge they had was scaling the

number of rainmakers they had at the firm. In law firms, for example, individuals finish law school, get a job, and it is several years before they discover that being a successful lawyer is not just about delivering quality work and winning cases. In some consulting companies the guys making all the money do not want the technician to be distracted by connecting and selling in the marketplace. The most successful firms do care because they understand that the end game is developing the trusted advisor role at their firm. The great aspect of technology today and the interconnectedness of the world is that we do not have to be an employee of a large firm to be a trusted advisor. If you build a network and take care to nurture it regularly, it will pay dividends.

Remember the story about the lumberjack who failed to sharpen his axe? Do not let your axe get dull. It is easy because as a knowledge worker, you love working on cool stuff, so delivery is the bomb. Do not forget that connecting, networking, and selling is like a set of different muscles that will atrophy if you do not exercise and work them. Read this book at least once a year and surround yourself with like-minded individuals who will push you towards success. Just like musicians, actors, and athletes go back to the basics each season or year, we all need reminders to get back to the basics.

Look for the blog and book at www.connectforlife.com.

Have fun and remember to connect for life! - John

Bibliography

Bitter, Alex. *"Bank of America Cuts Branches & Workers to Focus on $3 Billion-a-Day Mobile Business."* The Street.com. June 3rd, 2015.

Bosworth, Michael. *Solution Selling – Creating Buyers in Difficult Selling Markets.* New York: McGraw Hill, 1995.

Carnegie, Dale. *How to Win Friends and Influence People.* New York: Gallery Books (a division of Simon & Schuster, Inc.), 1936.

Daley, Kevin with Emmitt Wolfe. *Socratic Selling: How to Ask the Questions that Get the Sale.* New York: McGraw Hill, 1996.

DiModica, Paul. *Value Forward Selling.* Atlanta: Johnson & Hunter, 2006

Ellis, Joseph H. *Ahead of The Curve: A Common Sense Guide to Forecasting Business and Market Cycles.* Boston: Harvard Business School Press, 2005.

Grant, Adam. *Give and Take.* New York: Penguin Books, 2013.

Harding, Ford. *Creating Rainmakers – The Manager's Guild to Training Professionals to Attract New Clients.* Hoboken, NJ: John Wiley & Sons, Inc., 2006.

"Jon Huntsman Biography," Biography.com, accessed November 7th, 2016, https://www.biography.com/people/jon-huntsman-20719757

Mackay, Harvey. *Dig Your Well Before You're Thirsty.* New York: Doubleday, 1997.

U.S. Department of the Interior, *The Rockefeller Family, What They Gave*. National Park Service.

Page, Rick. *Hope is Not a Strategy: The Six Keys to Winning the Complex Sale*. Atlanta: Nautilus Press, Inc., 2002.

Rackham, Neil. *Spin Selling*. New York: McGraw Hill Book Company, 1988

Sanders, Tim. *Love is the Killer App: How to Win Business and Influence Friends*. New York: Crown Business, 2002

Schiffman, Stephan. *Cold Calling Techniques (That Really Work!)*. Holbrook, MA: Bob Adams Inc., 1990.

Ziglar, Zig. *Zigler on Selling*. 1991, Cambridge, OT: Oliver-Nelson Books, 1991

Made in the USA
Las Vegas, NV
16 February 2022

44019276R00129